REFLECTIONS

SPEECHES FROM THE HEART

ROB PECK

 FriesenPress

One Printers Way
Altona, MB R0G 0B0
Canada

www.friesenpress.com

ISBN
978-1-03-913222-1 (Hardcover)
978-1-03-913221-4 (Paperback)
978-1-03-913223-8 (eBook)

1. SELF-HELP, MEDITATIONS

Distributed to the trade by The Ingram Book Company

TABLE OF CONTENTS

ACKNOWLEDGEMENTS   V

FOREWORD   VI

PREFACE   VIII

1.   A PROBLEM—1997   1

2.   IF—1998   5

3.   WHO IS JESUS?   8

4.   REFLECTIONS ON DESIDERATA   13

5.   BREAD AND CIRCUSES—2001   17

6.   EMBRACING FAITH   22

7.   A TALE OF TWO FUNERALS   27

8.   WHAT I BELIEVE   30

9.   LIVING WITH FAITH   37

10. LOVE, GENTLENESS, AND PACE   42

11. REFLECTIONS ON RETIREMENT—2005   48

12. FINDING STRENGTH IN WEAKNESS   52

13. LOVE IS THE ANSWER   60

14. FIVE SECRETS TO MAKING A GREAT SPEECH (2008)   68

15. THE GOOD OLD DAYS—TAKE 1—DECEMBER 15, 2008   77

16. EULOGY FOR DAD—JANUARY 2009   81

17. WHY OFFICERS' TRAINING?   85

18. THE MOST IMPORTANT THING IN LIFE   91

19. HOW TO BECOME A BETTER SPEAKER   95

20. WHAT MAKES A GREAT SPEECH—TAKE 2   101

21. I ALWAYS WANTED TO LIVE FOREVER   103

22. TEN SLEEP CANYON   106

23.	"AHA!" MOMENTS	110
24.	LESSONS FROM JAPAN—2011	115
25.	THE GOOD OLD DAYS—TAKE 2—APRIL 11, 2011	120
26.	ARE YOU A GOOD NEIGHBOUR?	123
27.	CONVERSATION: WHAT DOES THE LORD REQUIRE OF YOU?	128
28.	UNCLE BRUCE	133
29.	WHY ST. MARK'S IS IMPORTANT TO ME	140
30.	PASTORAL CARE TRUMPS THEOLOGY	144
31.	HAPPY WIFE, HAPPY LIFE	149
32.	IN PRAISE OF KEEPING AT IT	155
33.	COLLEEN SMITH	163
34.	WHY I WRITE	169
35.	HOW TO WRITE A EULOGY	174
36.	THE GOODNESS OF HUMANITY	178
37.	THE GOOD OLD DAYS – TAKE 3 – 2017	183
38.	IN PRAISE OF IAN SCOTT MILLER	188
39.	CLARA MARGERY UPTON PECK	192
40.	GRATITUDE	195
41.	YOU WILL RISE!	200
EPILOGUE		204
ABOUT THE AUTHOR		207

ACKNOWLEDGEMENTS

To my wife, Julia, for her example of fierce caring for her family, her students, and the under-privileged;

To our children and grandchildren, for continually teaching me and reminding me of what is really important in life;

To Jim Hayhurst Sr., for reminding me what was important at a critical juncture in my journey when I might have been tempted in another direction;

To Ralph Smedley, for his gift of Toastmasters to the world;

To Ross Mackay, for his lifelong service to Toastmasters;

To Harold Patterson, for wrapping up his gifts and giving them away;

To all my friends in Toastmasters who have shared this path with me since 1969;

To my Mum and Dad, who loved me and persuaded me that I was important;

To the United Church of Canada, which has inspired me to look for the sacred in everyone and everything; and

To Donald Robertson, author of *How to Think Like a Roman Emperor*, for introducing me to Marcus Aurelius and Stoicism. Marcus Aurelius was a Roman emperor from 161 to 180 AD. However, Marcus was more concerned with his Stoic philosophy than with his role as emperor. He set down his philosophy in a series of reflections to himself, which have come down to us as his "Meditations." This book was inspired by Marcus. It is my "meditations."

FOREWORD

As a member of Toastmasters International for almost as long as the author, and as one who has undoubtedly delivered at least as many speeches, I now find myself feeling guilty of not collecting mine to the same extent. Although I have written a few books, each of them has focused on a single topic, so, consequently, the collection doesn't reveal much about me as an individual. In reading the collection of Toastmaster speeches that comprise the contents of his book, I was delighted to learn more about Rob Peck, a fellow Toastmaster whom I have admired for many years.

What I now know about him, that I didn't know before, is that this is a deeply spiritual being who has arrived at his beliefs by questioning and examining them in some depth and not simply by blindly accepting religious dogma as undisputed fact—the way so many others have done. I admire that greatly.

I also know that he adores his wife and family, he reveres and respects his fellow church members and Toastmasters' club members, and he loves and honours his friends, most of whom are included in the other groups.

In this intriguing book, Toastmasters particularly will appreciate the various topics of these speeches, which range from biblical commentaries to family events and a variety of other matters. This book is an example to all Toastmasters that your entire life is a speech topic just waiting to be considered and presented. I particularly related to his belief that every speech will benefit from being treated as an Ice Breaker, where one is required to introduce oneself to the members of their club. This very practical concept will help so many who struggle with how to approach the matter of writing a Toastmasters speech.

Many others will be able to take some valuable lessons from the philosophies expounded here when they too face some of the life struggles that Rob has shared with us.

I have also discovered that Rob has a great admiration for Maya Angelou, the American poet, author, and civil rights activist. His favourite quotation from her is:

> "People will forget what you said, people will forget what you did,
> but people will never forget how you made them feel."

It occurs to me that when an idea such as this is so close to your heart, it has become very much a part of who you are. Rob quotes that passage frequently.

I'm also told that one of the main reasons Rob is publishing this book is so that his children will get to know him better than they already might. There is no doubt that will happen. If my own experience is anything to go by, I would suggest that more than a few of his many friends are likely to benefit in exactly the same way.

This is a fascinating book for many different reasons, and I commend it to you wholeheartedly.

Ross C. Mackay, DTM, AS, PID

***

Ross Mackay is a professional speaker, entertainer, and author who has informed and inspired audiences in thirty-four countries around the world. He was a founding member of the Canadian Association of Professional Speakers and served four years on their Board of Directors. He has also been a member of Toastmasters International for almost thirty years, during which he served as District 60 Governor and on the International Board of Directors. In 2020 he was presented a Presidential Citation for outstanding and continued contributions to Toastmasters. In addition to writing his memoirs, Ross now enjoys entertaining senior citizen groups with his life-long love of music.

PREFACE

I was born to parents who travelled extensively for business and pleasure. My development was influenced by them, by our frequent moves, and by the churches we attended. When I grew up, I studied engineering and business administration.

Between my studies, I discovered Toastmasters International, a non-profit educational organization that teaches public speaking and leadership skills through a worldwide network of clubs. Off and on for over forty years since that first exposure, I have been a member of several different Toastmasters clubs. Every few months that I have been a member, I have presented a speech on subjects I found of interest. Typically, those speeches were about five to seven minutes long, which works out to approximately one thousand words.

The first formal prepared speech performed by a new Toastmaster is termed the "Ice Breaker." To make the new Toastmaster as comfortable as possible in this nerve-wracking experience, the Ice Breaker's subject is usually the person themselves. The thinking is that if you really know your subject, you will be more relaxed, and since the subject we all know best is ourselves, we should tell stories about ourselves.

It works. Ice Breakers are often fascinating speeches. Subsequent speeches in the Toastmasters' program emphasize different skillsets in speaking: organization, gestures, vocal variety, and the like. Often in doing these speeches, Toastmasters choose subjects about which they know little; they research a topic and give a speech laden with facts. The end result is a wooden, unenthusiastic presentation.

Over the years, I noticed that, frequently, Toastmasters get to their seventh or eighth formal speech before they again give a speech as good as their Ice Breaker. Why? Because they finally get back to choosing topics they care about and with which they have personal experience.

Then it hit me. Since the best speeches are Ice Breakers, we should strive to make *every* speech an Ice Breaker. After that, I started to make every speech I did an Ice Breaker. That is, every time I wrote a speech, I looked for how I could illustrate it with personal stories from my own life.

Harold Patterson, the 1987 World Champion of Public Speaking, talked about this in a superb article, "Wrap Up Your Package and Give It Away," in the September, 1988, *Toastmaster Magazine*. The following passages are excerpted from Harold's article:

> *To give a speech is to share a part of ourselves. Packaging knowledge with our own personal experience is like wrapping a gift: to share this package, to make a speech about this information, is to give the gift away. Past International Director Dick Schneider, DTM, encouraged me to personalize my speeches. This was probably one of the best suggestions I've ever received. I quit focusing solely on winning contests and started trying to share a little of myself. Trophy or not, win or lose, I always came up a winner because I had given a part of myself and done my very best. Ultimately, you must create the speech with which you feel most comfortable. When all is said and done, you must be able to say, "This is my speech. I believe in it, and I'm proud of it." If you can say this, you are a winner.*

I regularly reread Harold's article for inspiration and to recharge my batteries.

I have often used speech preparation as a way of working out my problems. If I have a problem, I write a speech about it. Many times, I find that by the time I have finished the speech, I have developed an approach to the problem.

I prepared most of my speeches for Toastmasters' exercises, but some as reflections for church services when I covered for the minister who was absent on vacation or study leave. Others were for other community events such as eulogies.

Initially, my speeches were in hard copy and I did not save them. However, since 1997, I have kept soft copies of most of my favourite speeches. That works out to over forty speeches, covering a period from 1997 to the present. These speeches are a record of my reflections over the past twenty-five years on the influences on my life, and on my personal philosophy, of my family, church, Toastmasters, friends, and world events.

Looking back over them, I can see where I have come from. That helps me determine where I still have to go. And whether I should change course!

I believe in them. I am proud of them. They are from the heart. In recent years, I have thought about publishing them as a book. The main idea is not to make money but to have a record, for my children, grandchildren, great-grandchildren, Toastmaster friends, and others, of who I was and what my interests were/are. If others could be helped by my recorded experiences, the things I tried that worked, and the things I tried that did not, so much the better!

This is that book. I am wrapping up my life in speeches and giving it away to whomever can use it! The speeches are arranged chronologically in the order in which I wrote them. While they have been tweaked in a few cases, they are essentially as originally written and presented. This has the advantage of showing how my speeches and personal philosophy have evolved over time.

One final point. You will notice that sometimes I have reused anecdotes in different speeches. There are good reasons for that. First, if a story is good, I feel it should not be thrown out after only one use, especially if it can be used again with a different audience! Second, a story might be used to good effect at different times in different ways to illustrate different points. Third, these speeches were often delivered at important times in my life; they accurately reflect my views at those times, and I do not want to rewrite history. Fourth, and most important, some points are important enough that they bear repeating! So, forgive me, I left the repetitions in!

Enjoy!

Rob Peck

Toronto, Canada
October 2021

CHAPTER 1

In February 1997, our children were twenty-two, twenty, eighteen, and seventeen years of age. I decided to share my wisdom gleaned from my previous ten years of dealing with teenagers.

A PROBLEM—1997

Ladies and gentlemen, with apologies to the Music Man:

We've got a problem
Right here in Toronto
And that starts with P and it rhymes with T
And <u>that</u> stands for … Teenagers.

How many people here have grown children or teenagers?

You can relax now. My speech is not for you. You already know everything I am about to say, so you can do something else for the next six minutes. Draw pretty pictures. Play cards or just go, "Blrrrrrrrrrrrrrb!" We'll understand!

How many people here have pre-teens?

God bless you! It is all about to happen. There is nothing that can be done for you. You are on the roller coaster. It is leaving the station; you can't get off. You <u>will</u> die! If you are masochist, stick around to hear what will befall you. If not, you are also excused. Go play with the first group—if you hear my talk, you will just get depressed.

How many of you have no children?

All right! On with the speech. This is for you! Especially the ladies! Listen, learn, and live!

What are teenagers?

The teenage years typically last about ten years, starting at age twelve and continuing until the subject is between twenty and twenty-five years of age. They are defined in terms of hormonal imbalance and actually bear no direct relationship to chronological age. Indeed, I am aware of one recorded case where the teenager is thirty-five years old, married, with two children of her own.

Why are they a problem?

It's all explained by the eighty-twenty rule. Twenty per cent of the people in this world cause eighty per cent of the mess. We call these people *teenagers*.

Most of them have parents. Recent studies have proven that, in a typical family with teenagers, twenty per cent of the people do eighty per cent of the work. These people are called mothers.

We call the people who do the remaining twenty per cent of the work fathers.

The teenagers do zilch! Nada! Rien! Comprenez? You capeesh? Teenagers feel that life is sooooo painful, they are justified in eating, sleeping, creating garbage, messing up their room, watching TV, and sighing about how hard done by they are! That is their raison d'être.

Why is this? Why does God do this to Her creatures? After all, She's a mother too, isn't she?

I talked to God about this, and She told me there were two reasons:

1. It's her punishment for us having too much sex!

2. It's her punishment for our having been teenagers in the past!

How can this wrong be corrected?

There are only three cures:

1. Suicide. The first option considered by most parents. This option is not recommended. It has a certain finality to it and arguably gives the teenager the sense that they have won. I hate that!

2. Murder. While a viable option, it carries a certain social stigma, as well as a period of incarceration that could last in excess of one or more golf seasons. Also not recommended.

3. Time. The preferred option. You have to wait it out. With any luck, they will grow up and have teenagers too. Then you get the last laugh.

So, to recap, we have a problem in Toronto. It's called teenagers. They are a problem because they make work for the rest of us.

There are three possible solutions to this problem:

1. Suicide is ruled out because it's giving in.

2. Murder is ruled out because it cramps our style.

3. Time ... the passage of time ... is the only viable course.

What should we do while we wait for time to work its healing wonders?

Prevention is the best course of action. If you don't have children, get sterilized or abstain from sex altogether. Monasteries and convents are good. So is hiking in Antarctica.

However, if you do have children, I recommend prayer. Monasteries and convents are good choices here as well. Failing those, church. This is likely the reason for the recent surge in church attendance as the children of Baby Boomers hit the teenage years.

Finally, remember what my dad always says: If I had known grandchildren were so much fun, I would have had them first!

Mr. Toastmaster.

CHAPTER 2

I have lived in Toronto since 1971. I married Julia in 1973, and we have attended church together since our children were baptized in 1979. Sometimes, the church needs a person to cover for a service when the minister is absent for vacation or study leave. In those cases, a member of the congregation is called upon to lead a service and give the related reflection. Such was the case in 1998, when I was board chair of our church, which at that time was West Hill United Church in Toronto.

IF—1998

The last few months have been challenging for me at work. Throughout this period, I have been sustained by the love of my family and the spiritual renewal I get from West Hill United Church (Sunday worship, our spiritual development class, the video study on contemporary Christian theologians and, yes, even board meetings!). Tom Bandy says our favourite hymn contains the clue to why we come to church. Like Jim Marshall, my favourite is "Amazing Grace." For me, that hymn says that, with all my faults, God loves me and will sustain me.

Many of the theologians our video group has studied over the past two months have said they no longer view God as a stern, old, bearded white patriarch dressed in a white robe. Now they see God as a "middle-aged Korean woman, very warm, very affirming, looking like my mother," or as a friend who lends them comfort when in need. I like that view of God. God often appears to me in the form of my friends at West Hill.

This past week, God appeared to me in the form of Rudyard Kipling's poem "If," with which many of you will be familiar. I repeat it here for the benefit of those who don't know it, as well as for the benefit of those who have seen it before. I personally could re-read it many times and not be bored by its message. I have taken the liberty of changing a few of Kipling's words to make the poem more inclusive.

If you can keep your head when all about you
Are losing theirs and blaming it on you,
If you can trust yourself when others doubt you,
But make allowance for their doubting too;
If you can wait and not be tired by waiting,
Or being lied about, don't deal in lies.

Or being hated, don't give way to hating,
And yet don't look too good, nor talk too wise:

If you can dream—and not make dreams your master;
If you can think—and not make thoughts your aim;
If you can meet with Triumph and Disaster
And treat those two impostors just the same.

If you can bear to hear the truths you've spoken,
Twisted by knaves to make a trap for fools,
Or watch the things you give your life to broken,
And stand and build them up with worn out tools.

If you can make one heap of all your winnings
And risk it on one turn of pitch-and-toss,
And lose, and start again at your beginnings
And never breathe a word about your loss.

If you can talk with crowds and keep your virtue,
Or walk with kings—nor lose the common touch,
If neither foes nor loving friends can hurt you,
If others count with you, but none too much;
If you can fill the unforgiving minute

With sixty seconds' worth of distance run,
Yours is the Earth and everything that's in it,
And—which is more—you'll have played the game and won!

Amen

CHAPTER 3

In 1998, as chair of the board of our church, I often thought about my religious views. What did I really believe? So I did a speech to my Toastmasters Club about it.

WHO IS JESUS?

The question seems to fascinate Christians and non-Christians alike. In recent years, it has been the subject of countless newspaper and magazine articles, radio and TV documentaries, musicals and movies.

Increasingly, books about the historical Jesus are becoming bestsellers.

Today, I am going to discuss why anyone would ask the question, how they might go about finding out the answer to the question once asked, and, finally, what scholars working in this field have concluded.

My speech is directed to those, Christian or non-Christian, who are open to listening to the debate. It is not my intent to embarrass or offend any who may be convinced that Jesus Christ is God, end of story. To those people, I can only say, "Forgive me, please. I'm sure that Jesus would!"

LET'S START. WHY WOULD YOU ASK WHO JESUS IS?

I personally have at least three reasons for asking.

First: Because, whether or not we are Christian, who we believe Jesus is informs much of who we believe God is.

Second: Because the traditional story of Jesus seems to me to be too fantastic to believe:

- God sends His son, Jesus, to offer his life as a sacrifice for our sins,

- a star leads three kings to his birthplace,

- his mother is a virgin,

- he walks on water and brings the dead back to life,

- after his death, he comes back to life, then is physically raised into heaven;

and, the part that I have the most trouble with,

- God will only forgive our sins if we believe this story.

My third reason for asking who Jesus is, is because we are allowed to. In other times and places:

- only the church could interpret the Bible,

- only priests could read and write,

- the church owned the universities, and

- people who didn't believe the official dogma were burned at the stake.

Today in Canada and many other parts of the world:

- most people can read,

- most universities are secular,

- people may believe and worship as they please,

- new discoveries shed new light on the subject; for example, the Nag Hammadi scrolls found in Egypt in 1945, and the Dead Sea Scrolls found in the Holy Land in 1948.

So, assuming that we wish to, how can we find out who Jesus is?

First, through comparative literary analysis. Through careful comparative study of the Gospels, and related Christian and secular writings of the time, scholars can see the early Christian authors at work, modifying and adding to the traditions they received.

Second, using modern sociological techniques, both cross-cultural and cross-temporal studies.

Finally, new archaeological discoveries shed new light on Jesus and the society of his day—notably, Nag Hammadi in Egypt and the Dead Sea Scrolls in Israel.

So what conclusions have scholars come to?

First, that the Gospels are not completely literally true. They are neither divine documents nor straightforward historical records. They are the church's memories of Jesus transformed by its experience and reflections in the decades after his death.

Second, scholars conclude we must distinguish between the "pre-Easter" and the "post-Easter" Jesus

The "pre-Easter" Jesus was a Jewish peasant who lived two thousand years ago.

His nature?

- He was grounded in the Spirit of God. He didn't just believe in God; he knew God intimately in a loving relationship. He called God, "Abba," the Aramaic word for Daddy.

- He was a teacher of wisdom, and

- He was world-affirming with a zest for life.

His skills?

- He was a charismatic speaker whose speech was poetic and filled with unique and powerful images and stories, often paradoxical, which challenged conventional wisdom;

- He was a brilliant debater who confounded his detractors; and

- He was a miraculous healer.

His message was about the nature of God:

- God loves you;

- Love your enemies; be compassionate as God is compassionate; forgive and you will be forgiven; God's realm is open to all, Gentile or Jew, slave or free, male or female, sinner or not, and, by implication, Black, white, yellow, red, or any combination thereof, homosexual or heterosexual;

- Religious life is about a deepening relationship with God, not about a life of requirements and reward.

For all of the above, he was crucified by the Roman authorities and his own people, and died.

The "post-Easter" Jesus is the Risen Christ, the Spirit that

- energized Jesus's followers after his death;

- persuaded them that he was still alive and with them;

- led many to conclude that Jesus was God.

The last conclusion that scholars have come to, which I want to present here, is that there is a dramatic difference between the religion of the pre-Easter Jesus and some of the religions about Jesus.

The religion of Jesus had much in common with the religion of Moses, the Buddha, Mohammed, Gandhi, Baha u llah, Indigenous people the world over, and of many other peoples who themselves have never even heard of Jesus.

Arguably, the religion of Jesus had more in common with those other religions than do some of the religions about Jesus that have developed in the past two thousand years.

In conclusion:

We ask "Who is Jesus?" because we can and we choose to.

We bring the latest techniques to bear on the question because they are the best we've got right now, and anything less would be insufficient.

Jesus may be God and he may not. What he was in the opinion of many scholars, and in my own, was a window on God. He knew God and conveyed that vision to those people fortunate enough to be in his presence.

God bless! But then, who is God?

Mr. Toastmaster!

CHAPTER 4

A speech I gave to Bay Street Breakfast Toastmasters in 1998.

REFLECTIONS ON DESIDERATA

The poem "Desiderata" was written and copyrighted in 1927 by Max Ehrmann, a lawyer and businessman in Terre Haute, Indiana, who was born in 1872 and died in 1945.

In the late 1950s, the poem was reproduced by Frederick Kates, the rector of Old St. Paul's Church in Baltimore, Maryland, along with other inspirational essays and poems that he had the habit of putting in the pews of the church. The church was founded in 1692. Rev. Kates reproduced the poem under the church's usual letterhead, "Old St. Paul's Church, AD 1692," which led to the common misconception that the poem itself dated back to 1692.

The rest is history. How many of you are familiar with it?

If you are, I suspect you won't mind hearing it again. If you aren't, I would like to correct that omission now. I would like to read it to you and share with you its meaning to me.

Go placidly amid the noise and the haste
and remember what peace there may be in silence.

**As far as possible without surrender
be on good terms with all persons.**

**Speak your truth quietly and clearly;
and listen to others,
even to the dull and the ignorant,
they too have their story.
Avoid loud and aggressive persons,
they are vexatious to the spirit.**

At work and at leisure, I seek out quiet, gentle people. It took me longer to decide to avoid loud and aggressive people. I am still working at this. I fear I may be considered loud and aggressive by some of the people I admire most.

**If you compare yourself with others,
you may become vain or bitter;
for always there will be greater and lesser persons than yourself.**

**Enjoy your achievements
as well as your plans.**

**Keep interested in your own career, however humble;
it is a real possession in the changing fortunes of time.**

This is a hard one for me. In my engineering class, my MBA class, and my circle of friends, there are many who have achieved greater material success than me. Even while I count my many blessings, I find myself wondering "Why?" "Why not?" and "What if?"

**Exercise caution in your business affairs,
for the world is full of trickery.
But let not this blind you to what virtue there is;
many persons strive for high ideals,
and everywhere life is full of heroism.**

Be yourself.

Especially do not feign affection.
Neither be cynical about love;
for in the face of aridity and disenchantment
it is as perennial as the grass.
Take kindly the counsel of the years,
gracefully surrendering the things of youth.

Many people in business are cynical. Some consider me a hopeless roman-
tic optimist, out of touch with the real world. This I can handle! I would
rather live in my world than in theirs.

Nurture strength of spirit
to shield you in sudden misfortune.

But do not distress yourself with dark imaginings.

Many fears are born of fatigue and loneliness.

Beyond a wholesome discipline,
be gentle with yourself.

You are a child of the universe,
no less than the trees and the stars;
you have a right to be here.

And whether or not it is clear to you,
no doubt the universe is unfolding as it should.

At first unconsciously, but now consciously, I have created for myself
islands of peace in the ocean of stress on which my little ship sails. Home
is one such island. West Hill United Church in Scarborough is another.
The GO train, believe it or not, is another. Lunch with Ian, Al, and Dave is
another. Bay Street Breakfast Toastmasters at 7:30 on Wednesday mornings is another, to name a few. I regularly dock in these safe harbours for
repairs or just for R and R. Then—repaired, rested, and refreshed—I take
my ship out of the harbour again and back to sea.

Therefore, be at peace with God,
whatever you conceive God to be.

**And whatever your labours and aspirations
in the noisy confusion of life,
keep peace in your soul.**

**With all its sham, drudgery and broken dreams;
it is still a beautiful world.**

Be cheerful. Strive to be happy.

At present, I see God in the sunrise on the GO train platform, in the Rocky Mountains on the Icefields Parkway between Banff and Jasper, in a Monarch butterfly, in my family, in my friends at church, and in my friends here at Toastmasters.

And I am happy.

Mr. Toastmaster.

CHAPTER 5

In 2001, Toronto was considering a bid for the Olympic Games. It was a hot topic with many of us! This was a speech I gave to Bay Street Breakfast Toastmasters in April 2001 on Toronto's bid for the 2008 Olympic Games.

BREAD AND CIRCUSES—2001

How many people here are in favour of the Olympic Games Movement? How many people are against the Olympics?

My purpose in speaking to you today is to persuade you, if you don't already, to support the Olympics.

It is not to get you to support Toronto's bid versus that of Beijing or Istanbul or Osaka or Paris.

My purpose is to persuade you to support the Olympic Movement itself.

First, let me talk to those of you who are opposed to staging the Olympic Games. Why are you against the Olympics? Think about it.

In my experience, the main reason people are against the Olympics is the same reason the group Bread Not Circuses is against staging the Olympics in Toronto.

These people are concerned about the plight of the hungry,

of the homeless, and
of the poorly clothed in society.

Spend money on bread, they say, not circuses.

Who can argue against bread for the poor? Who would want to? Certainly not I!

The problem I've got with the group Bread Not Circuses starts with the name: Bread Not Circuses.

That name for me conjures up the image of the Roman emperors who, instead of feeding their masses, organized grand spectacles in the Coliseum, where Christians were thrown to the lions, or gladiators were forced to fight each other to the death.

That name equates the Olympic Games with the Roman circuses.

That name also implies that we must make a choice between bread for the poor and the Olympic Games.

Ladies and gentlemen, the Games are not the Roman circuses, and you do not have to make a choice between feeding the poor and staging the Games.

I can think of at least three good reasons for supporting the Olympics:

First:

Jesus of Nazareth once said, "One does not live by bread alone."

He knew the truth that people experience a hunger that can't be filled merely by food and other material things. For life to be meaningful, people must concern themselves with things of the spirit as well as things of the flesh.

People need a higher purpose for living than simply to survive. If food were the only thing that was important, we might as well just be vegetables ourselves.

How many people here stayed up on December 31, 1999, to watch the people of different countries around the world welcome in the new millennium? Raise your hands!

Why did you do that? Was it perhaps because it thrilled you to feel connected with the rest of humanity? That's why I stayed up.

When I watch the opening ceremonies for each new Olympic Games, I feel that same thrill.

And when I watch the closing ceremonies and I hear the president of the International Olympic Committee say, "I call on the athletes of the world to assemble four years from now in Athens—or Beijing or Istanbul or Osaka or Paris or Toronto," I feel that same thrill.

I feel
that all good things are possible,
that good will triumph,
that people will love one another,
that we are all part of the same family, and
that excellence for the sake of excellence is a worthy goal.

Second:

In every city where the Olympics have been staged, the Olympics have been an energizer for getting things done. To take Toronto as an example, who can dispute that the city needs

Low-cost housing?
Improved transportation systems between the airport and the downtown?
Improved access to the waterfront?
Development of the waterfront?
Development of the railroad lands? and
Improved sports facilities for all of Toronto's citizens?

These things have been talked about for decades and little has been done. Now that the Toronto bid is seen to be real, the city, province, and country are cooperating to get them done!

Would that have happened without the bid? What do you think?

Third: To help the poor

Certainly, the plight of the poor needs to be addressed, regardless of whether the Olympics exist—in Toronto or elsewhere.

But staging the Olympics does not need to mean ignoring the poor. Indeed, it can be a vehicle for helping make the poor productive and healthy citizens.

The poor need jobs, not handouts. The Olympics will bring thousands of jobs to the city, the province, and the country. Not just for the three weeks that the Games are staged, but also for the years before when the new facilities are being planned and built, and for the years afterward when they are being operated and maintained.

Homeless, unemployed people can become middle-class tax-paying workers, rather than middle-class tax-paying workers becoming homeless unemployed.

So, in conclusion, let me recap:

By all means, let's have bread for our poor. But

1. Let's give them a reason to eat the bread! A reason to live! A vision of the family of mankind.

2. Let's energize the people of the city, province, and country that stage the Olympics to build a better world for people to live in, and

3. Let's give the poor jobs to build a better home for themselves and their families.

I call on the people of the world to support the Olympic Movement in Athens in 2004.

In Beijing or Istanbul or Osaka or Paris or Toronto in 2008.

Come together to celebrate our common humanity. To celebrate the best of the human spirit.

But don't forget the poor!

Because
we want,
we need,
we deserve

- Bread **and** Circuses!

Mr. Toastmaster

CHAPTER 6

In August 2002, I gave the following reflection.

EMBRACING FAITH

The following are actual quotes from church bulletins. Not West Hill's, I hasten to add!

1. Smile at someone who is hard to love. Say "hell" to someone who doesn't care much about you.

2. The church will host an evening of fine dining, superb entertainment, and gracious hostility.

And my personal favourite!

3. The Low Self-Esteem Support Group will meet Thursday at 7 p.m. Please use the back door!

In the scripture (Matthew 15: 21-28 New Revised Standard Version) that Jeanne read to us today, we heard the story of a Canaanite woman who came to Jesus seeking healing for her daughter. I think that woman could have related to these notices! Neither the disciples nor Jesus seemed to be acting in a Christian manner, did they?

Today, I want to look at that passage in some detail because I found it quite troubling.

First, I will look at each sentence in the scripture and give you my interpretation of what is being said. Then I'll give you my further reflections on the whole passage.

{21} Jesus left that place and went away to the district of Tyre and Sidon.

We know from the previous chapter that "that place" was Gennesaret, on the Sea of Galilee. Tyre and Sidon are about fifty miles northwest of Galilee in modern-day Lebanon, on the Mediterranean coast.

{22} Just then a Canaanite woman from that region came out and started shouting, "Have mercy on me, Lord, Son of David; my daughter is tormented by a demon."

"Canaanite" signified "pagan" to the Jews of Jesus's time. Most people who lived in the area of Tyre and Sidon were not Jewish.

However, it appears she knew something about Judaism and about Jesus. "Have mercy on me" is a cry of the afflicted often found in Scripture, especially in the Psalms. Her use of the title "Son of David" indicated that she recognized Jesus as the Messiah. It seems his fame had spread as far as Tyre and Sidon.

{23} But he did not answer her at all. And his disciples came and urged him, saying, "Send her away, for she keeps shouting after us." {24} He answered, "I was sent only to the lost sheep of the house of Israel."

At this point, Jesus described his mission as limited to the people of Israel. How different from what Matthew quotes Jesus saying at the end of his Gospel:

"… Go therefore and make disciples of all nations, baptizing them in the name of the Father and of the Son and of the Holy Spirit, and teaching them to obey everything that I have commanded you."

Whatever Jesus's reason or excuse was for saying this, my first reaction was acute disappointment. I find it difficult to reconcile Jesus's reaction to the Canaanite woman's cry for help with the Jesus who told the parable of the

Good Samaritan. What could Jesus have been thinking of? I can think of four possibilities:

1. Jesus meant exactly what he said. He was sent just to the Jews and had no interest in helping anyone else.

2. Jesus was tired and cranky. It had been a long day and he didn't have the patience he would have had had he been well rested.

3. Jesus didn't really mean what he said. He was testing her faith.

4. Jesus didn't really mean what he said. He let her go on with her behaviour to make a point with the disciples and others who were watching.

Who knows what really motivated him to act as he did? Your guess is as good as mine. I suspect it might have been a little bit of each of the above.

{25} But she came and knelt before him, saying, "Lord, help me."

The woman was obviously desperate. Why else would she dare approach a Jewish man? Jews had a rigid set of purity laws that governed their lives. Jews tried to avoid having to deal with pagans. Why, they would barely speak to the Samaritans! Besides that, women didn't ordinarily speak to strange men.

{26} He answered, "It is not fair to take the children's food and throw it to the dogs."

The nerve of the man! Yet she must have anticipated Jesus's rejection because she was quick to reply.

{27} She said, "Yes, Lord, yet even the dogs eat the crumbs that fall from their masters' table."

Some think the woman and Jesus must have been joking back and forth. It is hard to tell when we weren't there to see the body language or hear the tone of voice they were using. But would you joke like that with someone seeking help for her daughter who was deathly ill? The woman's acceptance of Jesus's insult only makes it seem harsher.

{28} Then Jesus answered her, "Woman, great is your faith! Let it be done for you as you wish." And her daughter was healed instantly.

Just like that! Jesus acquiesced and her daughter's health was restored.

So what is the message here? I take four things from this story:

1. The Importance of Faith

"Great is your faith," Jesus said. Compare this to the words he addressed to the apostle Peter in last week's Gospel: "You of little faith, why did you doubt?" Peter was a Jew, Jesus's friend, and one of the chosen twelve, yet this pagan woman had shown greater faith than Peter. And her faith was rewarded.

She had nothing except faith and courage and love of her child—faith and courage and love so great that they changed Jesus's mind. By acceding to her request, Jesus repudiated the Jews' purity doctrine.

2. Jesus's Humanity

Do we need Jesus to be so divine that we require him to know more than his historical and cultural location permitted? Whatever Jesus's motives were for initially refusing to help this woman, perhaps this story's significance lies in demonstrating Jesus's willingness to be converted by the woman.

3. The Importance of Persistence

In Matthew 7 verse 7, eight chapters earlier in this same Gospel, Jesus says, "Ask, and it will be given you; search, and you will find; knock, and the door will be opened for you."

The mother's unrelenting campaign to find an end to her daughter's torment forced Jesus to recognize her as one he had been sent to serve. The courage she demonstrated in setting aside her upbringing—her refusal to accept that she did not even deserve scraps from the table—not only led to her daughter's healing but revealed to Jesus another layer of meaning behind his own teachings.

And the message for us seems to be clear: "Don't take 'No' for an answer."

4. We Are All God's Children

The healing of the daughter of a Canaanite woman continues the question of including non-Israelites in the kingdom. At first, Jesus resisted her request, expressing what must have been a general feeling: "the gifts of God to the people of God." But she persisted, and at last, Jesus praised her for her great faith and healed her daughter.

Jesus set limits on what he was to do. Even Jesus did not expect to help everybody. But Jesus allowed those limits to be stretched by another's necessity. In other words, the rule here was that there was no rule, only a creative tension between our finite capacities and the world's infinite need.

"They'll know we are Christian by our love," the words of the song say. Not by hate. Not by fear. Not by excluding anyone.

We tend to draw circles where only "me and mine" belong. For example, "gated" communities are becoming more and more popular. The circles, some people think, will keep us safe. The circles will keep "them" out—whoever they may be.

But God keeps drawing bigger circles. God's circles are not meant to keep anyone out. God's circles are embraces that draw people in.

And isn't that a good thing for us all? If that weren't the case, we might risk finding ourselves on the outside.

The Canaanite woman teaches us that embracing faith yields amazing grace!

Amen

CHAPTER 7

A speech I gave to Bay Street Breakfast Toastmasters in May 2003.

A TALE OF TWO FUNERALS

Funerals stick in the memory. They are the worst of times. They are the best of times.

Funeral Defined

By funeral, we mean the post-death activities that may include any type of meaningful ceremony to commemorate the life of the deceased.

What's a funeral for?

A funeral or memorial service is for the living. It provides the setting and opportunity to celebrate a life that has been lived.

When a loved one dies, it is always a difficult time. Emotions run high. We may feel anger, confusion, sadness, or even feel emotionally numb. The funeral service is a way to bring caring people together—to lend support and to help each other through difficult times. The funeral helps confirm the reality and finality of death. It encourages mourners to face the pain of their loss and express their thoughts and feelings. It helps the survivors to better cope with their grief and enables them to move forward in their lives.

The funeral should meet the needs of the family. The service, whether religious in nature or not, may include personal readings, stories, or anecdotes about the deceased, eulogies by family members, and musical numbers of meaning to the family. However, death is both a private and a public matter. While the death of a family member is a very personal loss, that death also affects distant family, friends, and the community at large.

Julia's Dad's funeral. March 1991

Background

Julia's dad, Bob Buchanan, was insecure:

1. He only completed Grade 8 in school and always felt sensitive about that.

2. He had a congenital heart problem that led his family to expect he would not live to adulthood, so why waste the money on his education?

3. His father deserted the family when he was young, leaving his mother to raise the kids on her own.

He was a difficult man—if you did something foolish or questionable, he felt it only right to tell you about it … to your face! As a result, he did not have many friends; he changed jobs a lot, and the family moved a lot.

He was a good man. He cared deeply about people and especially about family. He was bitterly resentful of his father for deserting the family and doubtless resolved to never do the same to his family.

He was always faithful.

He was proud of his kids—unfortunately, he didn't know how to tell them. His daughter, Julia, recalls bringing home an exam that she got 85 per cent on. She proudly presented it to her dad, who said, "If you got 85 per cent on it, why couldn't you get 90 per cent? Or, better yet, 100?"

Funeral Ceremony

When Bob died in Ottawa in March of 1991, the funeral was sparsely attended. It was cold (it was the middle of the worst snowstorm of a cold Ottawa winter). Don Farnell did the eulogy. He talked about all the good things.

We really appreciated the effort taken by some friends and family to attend. We all mourned for what might have been.

Bob Cruikshank's funeral. July 2001

Background

Bob was quiet and secure in who he was.

He was a good man, a kind man. A geography teacher his whole career.

He had six kids, all salt of the earth.

Funeral Ceremony

The ceremony was a celebration of what was. It was filled to overflowing. It was on a warm summer day with the sun shining. There were many eulogies. Several were by the kids ... memories of time taken with family and friends. He was there for them.

He lived and worked in Scarborough his whole life.

Lessons I took from these funerals

1. Whoever dies with the most toys, still dies.

2. Live a good life. Like it or not, you are a role model.

3. Have people who really care participate.

4. Eulogies matter. They validate the life not only of the deceased but also of the living ... of those who loved the deceased.

CHAPTER 8

A reflection I gave in 2003 when our minister was on vacation.

WHAT I BELIEVE

FIRST, SOME BACKGROUND

1. **I Was Raised in the Church**

   We moved a lot when I was growing up. Every few years we were in a new town, usually in a new country. Physically and spiritually, I have always been on a journey.

   One thing that was constant, though, was church. Wherever we lived, we joined a nearby church and went there on Sunday. I went to Sunday School and learned the Bible stories, including, but not restricted to, the parables of the Prodigal Son and the Good Samaritan.

2. **The Prodigal Son**

   I remember in my teens, my parents said to me, "No matter what happens, remember, we love you. Nothing will ever change that. You can always come home."

   In the years that followed, those words have often come back to me. When I had to go away to school for Grade 13, when I went off to university, and when I went off to work, there were many times when the world seemed a difficult place, many times when I thought I would flunk out one way or another. Never in my darkest hour did I ever think I couldn't go home.

And that always meant a lot.

I have tried to remember that in my dealings with my own children. Saint Paul said it best:

"For I am convinced that neither death, nor life, nor angels, nor rulers, nor things present, nor things to come, nor powers, nor height, nor depth, nor anything else in all creation, will be able to separate us from the love of God in Christ Jesus our Lord."

That is my template, as it was my parents' before me. Our door is always open. The kids can always come home. Nothing will ever be able to separate them from our love.

3. The Good Samaritan

I met my wife, Julia, in 1972, thirty-one years ago this month. On our first real date, I took her to the Toronto production of *Godspell*, a musical based on the life of Jesus that was playing at the Royal Alex.

As we were about to enter the theatre, we were aware of a beggar accosting people outside the theatre. I was torn. Should I give him money or not? What would my date think of me if I did? What would she think of me if I didn't? I passed by on the other side feeling cheap and embarrassed.

Fifteen minutes later, we were sitting comfortably in our seats and the show started. Jesus came out on the stage. Guess who was the actor playing Jesus? Right the first time! The beggar from the front of the theatre!

Ever since then, the image of that beggar at the front of the theatre has been burned into my consciousness.

Fast forward to the present ...

I go to work every day on the GO train. On a typical day, as I walk between Union Station and Scotia Plaza, I will see two or three people begging for money.

That upsets me, especially in winter, when the people in question have obviously slept the night over the grates on the northeast corner of Bay and Wellington or in front of the Design Centre in the old stock exchange building.

That, I think, could be me there. What can I do to help them? If I put a toonie in their Tim Hortons coffee cup, will it help? And if I don't, what kind of a human being am I? And always I think of that beggar at the front of the theatre.

That is why I support our church and the Mission and Service Fund and the United Way and Habitat for Humanity.

WHAT I BELIEVE ABOUT GOD

I am an engineer by training, a banker by profession, and a skeptic of the first order. I like concrete things ... things I can touch and hold on to.

So in the year of our Lord 2003, what do I believe about God?

1. **I find the traditional story we get from the Gospels hard to believe:**

   - God comes to this planet to offer His life as a sacrifice for the sins of the world;

   - A star leads three kings to his birthplace;

   - His mother is a virgin;

   - He walks on water and raises the dead;

   - After his death, he comes back to life, then is physically raised into heaven;

And, the most incredible part of all,

- God (the same God of the Prodigal Son and the Good Samaritan) will only forgive all our sins if we believe this story!

2. **But then I find reality hard to believe:**

- Unseen signals in the ether are mysteriously converted into sounds from our radios and cell phones and pictures on our TVs;

- $E = MC^2$;

- Black holes the size of the moon have masses greater than five hundred of our suns;

- the universe, with billions of stars in each of billions of galaxies, started some 15 billion years ago from nothing.

So, God knows, I am not really sure what to believe! Which is part of the reason I enjoy our annual January-to-May book-study group because we study books, films, and videos that shed light on our faith and that of others.

My beliefs today reflect views I have assimilated from many different sources, including but not restricted to:

1. Tom Gilchrist, Bruce Sanguin, and Gretta Vosper, the ministers here at West Hill since Julia and I joined in 1986.

2. The authors we have studied since we started attending the Book Study in 1987, including John Dominic Crossan, Matthew Fox, John Shelby Spong, and Marcus Borg, among others.

3. Other members of the Book Study and the congregation of West Hill.

I believe that God is the ultimate source of life and that to worship God we must live fully and share deeply.

I believe that God is the ultimate source of love and that to worship God we must love wastefully, spread love frivolously, and give love away without stopping to count the cost.

WHAT I BELIEVE ABOUT JESUS

No human being I know of lived their life more fully, shared it more deeply, and loved more wastefully than did Jesus of Nazareth.

Neale Donald Walsch, in his book, *Conversations with God*, quotes God as telling him that God is our highest, best thought.

My highest, best thoughts always come back to the Prodigal Son and the Good Samaritan parables of Jesus.

I further believe:

1. **The Gospels—Matthew, Mark, Luke, and John—are not absolutely true.**

   I believe they are the developing traditions of the early Christian movement. They are the church's memories of the historical Jesus transformed by the community's experience and reflections in the decades after Easter.

2. **We should distinguish between the "pre-Easter" and the "post-Easter" Jesus**

   The "pre-Easter" Jesus was a Jewish peasant who lived two thousand years ago. The "post-Easter" Jesus is the Christ, the Spirit who has energized Jesus's followers for millennia after his death on a cross in Jerusalem.

   a. **The "Pre-Easter" Jesus**

      i. The "pre-Easter" Jesus didn't just believe in God, he knew God. He was:

         • Grounded in the Spirit of God;

- A teacher of wisdom who saw religious life as a deepening relationship with the Spirit of God, not as a life of requirements and reward;

- World-affirming with a zest for life.

ii. <u>He was brilliant,</u>

- A charismatic speaker whose speech was poetic and filled with unique and powerful images and stories;

- A skilled debater who confounded his detractors;

- A healer.

iii. <u>His message was about the nature of God, not about himself:</u>

- God loves you;

- Be compassionate as God is compassionate;

- Love your enemies;

- Forgive as you will be forgiven;

- God's kingdom is open to all, Gentile or Jew, slave or free, male or female, sinner or not, and, by implication, Black, white, yellow, red, or any combination thereof, homosexual or heterosexual.

iv. <u>The Roman authorities crucified him and he died.</u>

b. **The "Post-Easter" Jesus**

Is the Christ, the experience of the Spirit that:

- energized Jesus's followers after his death;

- persuaded them that he was still alive and with them;

- led many to conclude that Jesus was God, although many scholars doubt that Jesus believed or preached that himself.

3. **Difference between the religion of Jesus and the religion about Jesus**

I believe that the religion of Jesus had much in common with the religions of Abraham, the Buddha, Mohammed, Gandhi, Baha u llah, Indigenous people the world over, and many other peoples who themselves have never even heard of Jesus. I believe the religion of Jesus had more in common with those other religions than do some of the religions about Jesus that have developed in the past two thousand years.

CONCLUSION

Ralph Waldo Emerson said "success" was

To laugh often and much;

To win the respect of intelligent people
and the affection of children;
To earn the appreciation of honest critics and
endure the betrayal of false friends;

To appreciate beauty;

To find the best in others;

To leave the world a bit better, whether by
a healthy child, a garden patch, or a redeemed social condition;

To know even one life has breathed
easier because you have lived;

This is to have succeeded.

I believe that Jesus succeeded. Two thousand years later, Christians and non-Christians alike still look to him as a window on God and as a model on which to pattern their lives.

Thanks be to God!

Amen

CHAPTER 9

A reflection I gave in 2004.

LIVING WITH FAITH

I have always had questions. I've never had any answers. I have just had questions.

I think the first word I said was "Why?"

Later, my questions got bigger.

- What is God?

- What are we here for?

- What do I want to do when I grow up?

- Who cares?

- Is that all there is?

- What do we believe?

In my life to date, while I haven't had the answers to the questions that have plagued me, I have stumbled across four principles that have helped guide me:

1. *<u>The Golden Rule</u>* The Golden Rule is in every religion. The full list is too lengthy for today's reflection, but some examples illustrate the point:

Judaism: What is hateful to you, do not to your fellow man. That is the entire law; all the rest is commentary.

Talmud, Shabbat 31a—thirteenth century BC.

Buddhism: Hurt not others in ways that you yourself would find hurtful.

Udana-Varga 5:18—fifth century BC.

Brahmanism (Hinduism): This is the sum of duty: Do naught unto others which would cause you pain if done to you.

Mahabharata 5:1517—third century B.C.

Christianity: So, in everything, do to others what you would have them do to you, for this sums up the Law and the Prophets.

Matthew 7:12—first century A.D.

Islam: No one of you is a believer until he desires for his brother that which he desires for himself.

Sunnah—seventh century A.D.

Surely somebody is trying to tell us something! These words have guided mankind since prehistory!

2. (From William Shakespeare's play *Hamlet*.) ***This above all, to thine own self be true, and it must follow, as the night the day, thou canst not then be false to any man.***

This was Polonius's advice to his son, Laertes, as he left for the bright lights of Paris. Since the day I played Polonius in a high school production of *Hamlet*, I have remembered those words and tried to live by them.

3. (From Viktor Frankl's wonderful book, *Man's Search for Meaning*): *Success, like happiness, cannot be pursued; it must ensue, and it only does so as the unintended side effect of one's personal dedication to a cause greater than oneself.*

Frankl's book tells the story of his journey through the Nazi death camps during World War II and the lessons he learned from his fellow inmates—most particularly, how some inmates were able to survive the experience when other, apparently much stronger, people were not.

4. *Relish the moment*

Robert Hastings' *The Station* is all about forgetting the destination and enjoying the ride.

The Station

Tucked away in our subconscious is an idyllic vision. We are travelling by train—out the windows, we drink in the passing scenes of children waving at a crossing, cattle grazing on a distant hillside, row upon row of corn and wheat, flatlands and valleys, mountains and rolling hillsides and city skylines. But uppermost in our minds is the final destination. On a certain day, we will pull into the station.

Bands will be playing and flags waving. Once we get there, our dreams will come true and the pieces of our lives will fit together like a completed jigsaw puzzle. Restlessly we pace the aisles, damning the minutes—waiting, waiting, waiting for the station. "When we reach the station, that will be it!" we cry. "When I'm eighteen." "When I buy a new Mercedes-Benz SL 450!" "When I put the last kid through college!" "When I have paid off the mortgage!" "When I get a promotion!" "When I reach retirement, I shall live happily ever after!"

Sooner or later, we realize there is no station, no one place to arrive. The true joy of life is the trip. The station is only a dream. It constantly outdistances us. "Relish the moment" is a good motto, especially when coupled with Psalm 118:24: "This is the day which the Lord hath made; we will rejoice and be glad in it."

It isn't the burdens of today that drive men mad. It is the regrets over yesterday and the fear of tomorrow. Regret and fear are twin thieves who rob us of today. So stop pacing the aisles and counting the miles. Instead, climb more mountains, eat more ice cream, go barefoot more often, swim more rivers, watch more sunsets, laugh more, cry less. Life must be lived as we go along. The station will come soon enough.

My Life from Now On

I am now fifty-eight. I still wrestle with the same questions that flummoxed me at fifteen, at twenty-five, and at forty!

- What is God?

- What are we here for?

- What do I want to do when I grow up?

- Who cares?

- Is that all there is?

- What do we believe?

But I don't worry about the answers any more.

Because I have learned that they change! The questions stay the same, but the answers always change! Look at the Apostles' Creed, followed by the New Creed of the United Church of Canada, and now the most recent discussions in West Hill United as to what we believe.

Today, I care less about the goal and more about the journey.

Looking back, I realize that I have always lived my life on faith—faith that living life according to the principles I value is important. Not because it will make me richer, or that it will guarantee that I will never be sick, but because it is the right thing to do.

The letter to the Hebrews says:

"Now faith is the assurance of things hoped for, the conviction of things not seen. Indeed, by faith our ancestors received approval. By faith we understand that the worlds were prepared by the word of God, so that what is seen was made from things that are not visible."

Micah says, "He has told you, O mortal, what is good; and what does the LORD require of you but to do justice, and to love kindness, and to walk humbly with your God?"

My bottom line—the best part of every religion is in every other religion. So have faith. Listen to your heart and act accordingly.

As for me, I'm taking up golf! Gord, sign me up for the Prayer's Championship in 2005!

Amen

CHAPTER 10

A reflection I gave in the summer of 2005.

LOVE, GENTLENESS, AND PACE

OPENING

Recently, a friend spoke to me about the stress he was under. I'll call him John. That is not his real name. Week after week, month after month, John feels under pressure. His marriage broke down because he would come home from work after his wife had fallen asleep and would leave for work before she woke up in the morning. On those occasions that they were both home and awake at the same time, they would argue about the amount of time he spent at work.

I wonder how many of us can relate in some measure to his predicament, either because it is, or has been, our own, or because it is that of a spouse, a parent, or a friend or relative.

Our Gospel reading for today speaks directly to this issue:

Jesus said:

28 "Come to me, all you that are weary and are carrying heavy burdens, and I will give you rest.

29 Take my yoke upon you, and learn from me; for I am gentle and humble in heart, and you will find rest for your souls.

30 For my yoke is easy, and my burden is light."

I want to look at those few verses from Matthew for the next ten minutes.

BODY

A. First, the problem

Jesus said:

28 "Come to me, all you that are weary and are carrying heavy burdens, and I will give you rest."

Why are we weary and carrying heavy burdens? Two reasons occur to me:

1. We want the wrong things … and more of them!!

2. We try to do too much … we don't schedule enough downtime— time to reflect, time to meditate … time to listen to others … time to just _be_ with others.

This begs a whole bunch of questions. Why do we work? Is it to get more status? To get that promotion? Then what? The next promotion? And the next?

Is it to get more money? For what? A better house? A boat? A cottage?

Because, if it is for those reasons we work,
and
if, as a result of working long hours for those reasons we neglect ourselves, our families, our relationships, and our spiritual lives, then, Houston, we have a problem!

John, the friend I spoke of, has a problem. On the one hand, he has a job that gives him all the money he wants and that gives him the status he wants.

On the other hand,

a. Even though he has always received superior performance reviews, his job is so complex that he lives in constant physical fear of making a mistake that will see him fired.

b. He lives next door to his parents, and he hasn't seen them for two weeks.

c. He loves his nephews and nieces. Recently, they asked their mother why Uncle John never comes to see them anymore.

d. He envies me my wife, my children, my friends, my life.

B. Then, the solution!

Jesus has the answer to John's problem.

He said:

29 "Take my yoke upon you, and learn from me; for I am gentle and humble in heart, and you will find rest for your souls.

30 For my yoke is easy, and my burden is light."

Let's look at those words again …

1. **Take my yoke upon you**

Yoke is defined by Webster's as: A contrivance for joining together a pair of draft animals usually consisting of a crosspiece with two bow-shaped pieces enclosing the head of an animal.

I believe it meant the same thing in Jesus's day.

Jesus says he is in the yoke with us. He doesn't ask us to pull alone. He will share the load with us. He will teach us ways to make the load lighter.

2. **"And learn from me**

   **For I am gentle and humble in heart
   and you will find rest for your souls.
   For my yoke is easy, and my burden is light."**

What did Jesus do? What did he say?

   i. **He knew what was important**

   Before Jesus appeared in the Bible, Micah had God's requirements down to a fairly small number:

   Micah 6:8

   "He has told you, O mortal, what is good; and what does the Lord require of you but to do justice, and to love kindness, and to walk humbly with your God?"

   Jesus agreed with Micah that less was more. Forget all the rules in Leviticus, Jesus said. Don't even worry about remembering all of Moses' ten commandments.

   Matthew 22

   When the Pharisees heard that he had silenced the Sadducees, they gathered together, and one of them, a lawyer, asked him a question to test him: "Teacher, which commandment in the law is the greatest?" He said to him, "'You shall love the Lord your God with all your heart, and with all your soul, and with all your mind.' This is the greatest and first commandment. And a second is like it: 'You shall love your neighbour as yourself.' On these two commandments hang all the law and the prophets."

   ii. **He had a gentle approach**

   There is so much talk about assertiveness training these days. Be aggressive. Demand your rights.

   Jesus originated the passiveness training program.

Look at the Beatitudes:

Matthew 5

"Blessed are the poor in spirit, for theirs is the kingdom of heaven.
"Blessed are those who mourn, for they will be comforted.
"Blessed are the meek, for they will inherit the earth.
"Blessed are the merciful, for they will receive mercy.
"Blessed are the pure in heart, for they will see God.
"Blessed are the peacemakers, for they will be called children of God."

So much of what we do today seems to involve confrontation, noise, aggression.

This takes a toll on us all—on the aggressor and the aggressee. We find fault and we punish, and the punished find fault with the punisher, and the cycle continues.

Jesus asks us to break the cycle. Don't punish, forgive. Don't hate, love.

iii. He paced himself. He would take one step at a time

After a particularly busy period, he would leave the crowds and go off on his own to pray. He took the time to maintain his relationships with God and with his friends.

Matthew 6

Jesus says,

"Therefore, I tell you, do not worry about your life, what you will eat or what you will drink, or about your body, what you will wear. Is not life more than food, and the body more than clothing? Look at the birds of the air; they neither sow nor reap nor gather into barns, and yet your heavenly Father feeds them. Are you not of more value than they? And can any of you by worrying add a single hour to your span of life? And why do you worry about clothing? Consider the lilies of the field, how they grow; they neither toil nor spin, yet I tell you, even Solomon in all his glory was not clothed like one of these.

"Therefore, do not worry, saying, 'What will we eat?' or 'What will we drink?' or 'What will we wear?' But strive first for the kingdom of God and his righteousness, and all these things will be given to you as well. So do not worry about tomorrow, for tomorrow will bring worries of its own. Today's trouble is enough for today."

Many years later, Mark Twain paraphrased that, saying: "I've been through some terrible things in my life … some' of which actually happened!"

CONCLUSION

In conclusion, are you weary and heavy-laden? Why? Could it be that you are working for the wrong reasons? Could it be that you are trying to do too much?

If your answer to either of these questions is yes, then I suggest you come to Jesus, and he will give you rest.

Take his yoke upon you and learn from him:

a. Figure out what is important to you and stick to it. I would suggest you consider Jesus's Great Commandment in this regard: Love the Lord your God with all your heart and soul and strength, and your neighbour as yourself.

b. Be gentle

c. Pace yourself. Take time to be holy. Speak often with the Lord.

For he is gentle and humble in heart and you will find rest for your soul. For his yoke is easy and his burden is light.

Amen

CHAPTER 11

I retired on July 31, 2005. On September 4, I used the occasion as the basis of a reflection I gave when our minister was on vacation.

REFLECTIONS ON RETIREMENT—2005

As many of you know, I retired on July 31 after thirty-four years of working for my employer, a Canadian chartered bank.

Everywhere I go these days, people are asking me the same question: So, Rob, how's retirement? How does it feel?

What can I say? I've only been retired for a month. That is the length of a good vacation. I'm not retired yet, really. I am still on vacation.

If you really want to know what retirement is like, ask somebody with experience, like Glen Cockwell or Lloyd Wilson or Jeanne Hamel or Les Spurrier or Gord Ramsay.

But while I don't truly know what retirement is like yet, I do have some thoughts on the subject, which I will share with you this morning.

Carol Kilby has a workshop entitled "Work Like You Don't Need the Money." I never took the workshop, but ever since it was mentioned in church last year, I have often reflected on the title.

Working like you don't need the money truly is the ideal for all of us.

I fell into my job at the bank. My dreams about working in a job I loved gradually disappeared after graduation. Instead, I took a job where people would pay me enough money to pay the rent. It seemed like a good idea at the time.

When I married Julia, and then David, Ross, Jennifer, and Douglas came along, it seemed like an even better idea!

However, if you have a pension plan and/or RRSPs, once you retire, working like you don't need the money starts to seem achievable.

What do we mean by "retire"?

I think there is a difference between retiring *from* and retiring *to*.

"Retiring from" has slightly negative connotations, suggesting that we are getting old and decrepit and sick and are no longer of interest to our employer.

"Retiring to" is more positive in tone, in my opinion. It implies that **we** are choosing to withdraw from one vocation and to spend our time in different ways than heretofore.

To be frank, I started retiring *to* things other than the bank in 1989, sixteen years before I retired *from* the bank.

That year, we took a four-week vacation out west. During those four weeks:

- I saw that I could afford to live in much of Canada or the United States for a fraction of what it would cost in Toronto, and

- I got the bank completely out of my system. I mean, I forgot about it while I was away, and when I got back, I just couldn't muster up any interest in banking anymore.

That gave me options. For the first time, I felt that if the bank were to decide they could do without me, I could survive. Heck, I could thrive!

And I reflected on today's scripture reading from Matthew:

"And can any of you by worrying add a single hour to your span of life? And why do you worry about clothing? Consider the lilies of the field, how they grow; they neither toil nor spin, yet I tell you, even Solomon in all his glory was not clothed like one of these."

It was about this time, too, that I first read *The Station* by Bob Hastings.

Between the vacation, Matthew's comment on the lilies, and Bob Hastings urging us to enjoy the journey and forget about the destination, my life was irrevocably changed.

Thereafter, I put in my regular days at the bank, but I no longer felt motivated to put in ten hours a day, six days a week, the way I often had before.

I got more active in my other loves:

- in church,

- in Toastmasters

- and, lately, in running.

More particularly, I got more interested in living for today and less interested in sacrificing today for a possible reward tomorrow.

Last week, a member of the congregation sent me a lovely card honouring my retirement. Let me read it to you:

It's time to …

Refresh your spirit
Relax your body
Recall your success
Recharge your energy
Reflect on your contributions
Renew your friendships
Rejuvenate your mind
Remember your dreams

Reward yourself …
It's time for **you.**

That is a lovely card. I treasure the thoughts in it as I treasure the friend who sent it to me. But I think these thoughts are too important to wait for retirement.

Today is the day that the Lord has made! Rejoice and be glad **today**! Don't wait for tomorrow!

Admittedly, some planning is necessary. If you don't have a pension plan, and/or if you don't have any RRSPs, then when you come to the age of sixty or sixty-five, you might be financially unable to retire from or to anything.

But don't plan for tomorrow so much you forget to live today.

Whether you are six or sixty,

Whether you are twenty-five or ninety-five,

> **Today** is the time to …

> Refresh your spirit
> Relax your body
> Recall your success
> Recharge your energy
> Reflect on your contributions
> Renew your friendships
> Rejuvenate your mind
> Remember your dreams
> Reward yourself …
> It's time for **you.**

So climb more mountains, eat more ice cream, go barefoot more often, swim more rivers, watch more sunsets, laugh more, cry less. Life must be lived as we go along. The station will come soon enough.

Amen

CHAPTER 12

A reflection I gave on May 7, 2006, while our minister, Gretta, was away on other business.

FINDING STRENGTH IN WEAKNESS

Acts 4:5–12

The next day their rulers, elders, and scribes assembled in Jerusalem, with Annas the high priest, Caiaphas, John, and Alexander, and all who were of the high-priestly family. When they had made the prisoners stand in their midst, they inquired, "By what power or by what name did you do this?" Then Peter, filled with the Holy Spirit, said to them, "Rulers of the people and elders, if we are questioned today because of a good deed done to someone who was sick and are asked how this man has been healed, let it be known to all of you, and to all the people of Israel, that this man is standing before you in good health by the name of Jesus Christ of Nazareth, whom you crucified, whom God raised from the dead. This Jesus is 'the stone that was rejected by you, the builders; it has become the cornerstone.'

There is salvation in no one else, for there is no other name under heaven given among mortals by which we must be saved."

Psalm 23

The Lord is my shepherd, I shall not want. He makes me lie down in green pastures; he leads me beside still waters; he restores my soul. He leads me in right paths for his name's sake. Even though I walk through the darkest valley, I fear no evil; for you are with me; your rod and your staff—they comfort me.

You prepare a table before me in the presence of my enemies; you anoint my head with oil; my cup overflows. Surely goodness and mercy shall follow me all the days of my life, and I shall dwell in the house of the Lord my whole life long.*

John 3: 16–24

For God so loved the world that he gave his only Son, so that everyone who believes in him may not perish but may have eternal life.

Indeed, God did not send the Son into the world to condemn the world, but in order that the world might be saved through him. Those who believe in him are not condemned; but those who do not believe are condemned already, because they have not believed in the name of the only Son of God. And this is the judgement, that the light has come into the world, and people loved darkness rather than light because their deeds were evil. For all who do evil hate the light and do not come to the light, so that their deeds may not be exposed. But those who do what is true come to the light, so that it may be clearly seen that their deeds have been done in God.

After this Jesus and his disciples went into the Judean countryside, and he spent some time there with them and baptized. John also was baptizing at Aenon near Salim because water was abundant there; and people kept coming and were being baptized— John, of course, had not yet been thrown into prison.

FINDING STRENGTH IN WEAKNESS

This is another chapter in my own personal faith journey. I apologize if that offends anyone. My only defence is that I am not the theologian that Gretta is. What I can offer is some insight into where I am in my faith journey. Maybe that is relevant to you and yours. I hope so. If not, at least you will have a better idea of where I'm at right now.

PAUL'S WEAKNESS

In the passage from Paul's second letter to the church at Corinth read to us today by Jeanne, Paul says:

"… to keep me from being too elated, a thorn was given me in the flesh, a messenger of Satan to torment me, to keep me from being too elated.

Three times I appealed to the Lord about this, that it would leave me, but he said to me, 'My grace is sufficient for you, for power is made perfect in weakness.' So, I will boast all the more gladly of my weaknesses, so that the power of Christ may dwell in me."

MY WEAKNESS

I suspect that if we were to be truthful, we would all admit many personal weaknesses, thorns in our flesh, that keep us from being too elated.

What?

One of my weaknesses is that I have had trouble accepting John 3:16: "**For God so loved the world that he gave his only Son, so that everyone who believes in him may not perish but may have eternal life.**"

Why is this a weakness?

Many (maybe most?) Christians revere John 3:16 as the gospel within the gospel, the heart of the Christian message.

But the passage has troubled me because I feel it has been used by many avowed Christians to justify the forced conversion to Christianity of Jews, Muslims, native peoples, and other people of faith. The native peoples' treatment in residential schools run by Canadian churches on behalf of the Canadian government is one example that comes to mind.

I revere Jesus as a spiritual person with an awareness of the Divine unequalled in human history, with the possible exception of Siddhartha Gautama, the Buddha. While I acknowledge Jesus to be a son of God, I am not convinced he is the only son of God or that he is, or was, God incarnate.

I hasten to add that I don't know that he isn't and that I am speaking only for myself.

But if I didn't believe this passage to be the heart of the gospel, what kind of a Christian was I?

To me, for many years the heart of Jesus's message was his Great Commandment. As recorded in Luke, Chapter 10: "a lawyer stood up to test Jesus. 'Teacher,' he said, 'what must I do to inherit eternal life?' Jesus said to him, 'What is written in the law? What do you read there?' The lawyer answered, **'You shall love the Lord your God with all your heart, and with all your soul, and with all your strength, and with all your mind; and your neighbor as yourself.'** (emphasis added) And Jesus said to him, 'You have given the right answer; do this, and you will live.'"

To me these two passages were always separate and at odds with each other.

The first, John 3:16, I thought said if you wanted to go to heaven, you had to believe that Jesus was/is the Son of God, and indeed was God as part of the Trinity: Father, Son, and Holy Spirit.

The second said you had to love God and love your fellow human beings.

> The first required faith.
> The second required love.
> The first I found hard.
> The second I found much easier.

WHY WOULD I THINK OF THIS NOW?

Most churches worldwide, West Hill United included, follow a three-year list of scripture passages. This is called the lectionary. Each Sunday has a different group of passages from which ministers are expected to preach.

Understand that John 3:16 has come up twice in the lectionary this year, once on Good Friday and once on June 17.

Understand that this is rare. Most readings in the lectionary only occur once in every three-year cycle. Indeed, until this year, I thought all passages occurred only once in the three-year cycle.

Understand that my name is down to read Scripture on Sundays. I am one of about fifteen readers, which means I have a one-in-fifteen chance of reading any given passage on Sunday.

On the Wednesday before Good Friday, Gretta led a lectionary discussion of John 3:16, and I told her how I disliked it. I think she was surprised that I knew it off by heart.

Does anybody here ever watch NFL football on television? You will know why I knew it. At many of the games there is a chap with a big sign with "John 3:16" written in large block letters. I looked it up:

"For God so loved the world that he gave his only Son, so that everyone who believes in him may not perish but may have eternal life."

Well, after telling Gretta how much trouble I had with the passage, guess whose name came up in the schedule to read it on Good Friday? Right … the first time! Me. I tried to get out of it. I tried to get Gretta to let me introduce it by saying I had trouble with this one. No dice. She wasn't playing.

Well, two months later, Gretta calls me in stitches. Guess what passage is coming up on Sunday? John 3:16. Guess whose name came up in the roster to read it? Yours truly!

Coincidence? I think not!

Human intervention? Gretta and Peggy both plead innocent of all charges. Somebody is trying to tell me something, and it apparently is not Gretta or Peggy.

SO WHAT IS THE ANSWER?

So I was right there where Paul was when he talked to God about his weakness.

As Paul said in today's reading: "Three times I appealed to the Lord about this, that it would leave me, but he said to me, 'My grace is sufficient for you, for power is made perfect in weakness.'"

Three times I had tried to deny this scripture. Three times I was told to look at it again.

OK. I gave up. I looked at it again! I know when I'm beaten!

And then I remembered the words used by Marcus Borg on the last page of his book, *Meeting Jesus Again for the First Time* (you might recall this is the book that our Book Study group studied last year):

"I want to close by talking about a very familiar Christian phrase—believing in Jesus ... For those of us who grew up in the church, believing in Jesus was important. For me, what that phrase used to mean, in my childhood and into my early adulthood, was 'believing things about Jesus.' To believe in Jesus meant to believe what the gospels and the church said about Jesus. That was easy when I was a child, and became more and more difficult as I grew older.

"But I now see that believing in Jesus can (and does) mean something very different from that. The change is pointed to by the root meaning of the word *believe*. *Believe* did not originally mean believing a set of doctrines or teachings; in both Greek and Latin, its roots mean 'to give one's heart to.' The 'heart' is the self at its deepest level.

"*Believing*, therefore, does not consist of giving one's mental assent to something, but involves a much deeper level of one's self.

"*Believing* in Jesus does not mean believing doctrines about him. Rather, it means to give one's heart, oneself at its deepest level, to the post-Easter Jesus who is the living Lord, the side of God turned toward us, the face of God, the Lord who is also the Spirit."

SO ... MY CONCLUSION?

My definition of a Christian—that is, someone who gives his heart to Jesus's commandment to **"love the Lord your God with all your heart, and with all your soul, and with all your strength, and with all your mind; and your neighbor as yourself"**—does not conflict with Paul's statement, **"For God so loved the world that he gave his only Son, so that everyone who believes in him may not perish but may have eternal life."**

Because if you can do the first—and let's admit that is a challenge—you have given your heart to Jesus and you believe in him.

My weakness is my strength!

weaknesses can often be strengths

What is your biggest weakness? Could it in fact be a strength?

1. If Terry Fox had not had cancer, would you have heard of him? Would the world be a better place today?

And,

2. If Paul had not had his weakness, would he have still been motivated to found the Christian churches around the Mediterranean that have grown over the years into the church as we know it today?

Do you have a thorn in your flesh? Is there some aspect of your life that has caused you pain? Something that has significantly disrupted your life that you had not planned and did not wish for? More particularly, some burden that you have prayed or wished could be taken from you? Can you relate to Paul when he says, "Three times I appealed to the Lord about this, that it would leave me"?

58

And has God said, in one way or another, "My grace is sufficient for you, for power is made perfect in weakness. Deal with it?"

If so, like Terry Fox, like Paul, see what you can do to turn a weakness into a strength.

Then you can say with Paul:

"Therefore, I am content with weaknesses, insults, hardships, persecutions, and calamities for the sake of Christ; for whenever I am weak, then I am strong."

Amen

CHAPTER 13

A reflection I gave at church on August 27, 2006.

LOVE IS THE ANSWER

Scripture Readings for August 27, 2006

Micah 6:8

"He has told you, O mortal, what is good; and what does the Lord require of you but to do justice, and to love kindness, and to walk humbly with your God?"

John 10 10b–16

"I came that they may have life, and have it abundantly.

I am the good shepherd. The good shepherd lays down his life for the sheep.

The hired hand, who is not the shepherd and does not own the sheep, sees the wolf coming and leaves the sheep and runs away—and the wolf snatches them and scatters them. The hired hand runs away because a hired hand does not care for the sheep.

I am the good shepherd. I know my own and my own know me, just as the Father knows me and I know the Father. And I lay down my life for the sheep. **I have other sheep that do not belong to this fold. I must bring** them also, and they will listen to my voice. So, there will be one flock, one shepherd." (emphasis added)

John 13:34–35

"I give you a new commandment, that you love one another. Just as I have loved you, you also should love one another. By this everyone will know that you are my disciples, if you have love for one another."

1 John 4:19–21

"We love because he first loved us. Those who say, 'I love God,' and hate their brothers or sisters, are liars; for those who do not love a brother or sister, whom they have seen, cannot love God, whom they have not seen. The commandment we have from him is this: those who love God must love their brothers and sisters, also."

People's Witness

Martin Luther King Jr., on receiving his Nobel Peace Prize in 1964:

Sooner or later all the people of the world will have to discover a way to live together in peace, and thereby transform this pending cosmic elegy into a creative psalm of brotherhood. If this is to be achieved, man must evolve for all human conflict a method that rejects revenge, aggression, and retaliation. The foundation for such a method is love ... I believe that unarmed truth and unconditional love will have the final word in reality. This is why right temporarily defeated is stronger than evil triumphant. I believe that even amid today's motor bursts and whining bullets, there is still hope for a brighter tomorrow. I believe that wounded justice, lying prostrate on the blood-flowing streets of our nations, can be lifted from this dust of shame to reign supreme among the children of men.

I have the audacity to believe that peoples everywhere can have three meals a day for their bodies, education and culture for their minds, and dignity, equality, and freedom for their spirits. I believe that what self-centred men have torn down, men other-centred can build up. I still believe that one day mankind will bow before the altars of God and be crowned triumphant over war and bloodshed, and non-violent redemptive goodwill proclaim the rule of the land. "And the lion and the lamb shall lie down together and every man shall sit under his own vine and fig tree and none shall be afraid." I still believe that We Shall Overcome!

LOVE IS THE ANSWER

The media have been filled for the past several months with reports of the indiscriminate killings going on in Lebanon and Gaza. It has almost drowned out the stories in the media every day of the indiscriminate killings that have been going on in Iraq and Afghanistan. And the Sudan. And on and on and on.

Why do we do this to ourselves?

One of my most vivid images of war is that of Christmas in the trenches in 1914 when, for one all-too-brief period, soldiers from both sides sang "Stille Nacht" and exchanged holiday greetings.

The following is one account of the events:

On Christmas Day, 1914, only five months into World War I, German, British, and French soldiers, already sick and tired of the senseless killing, disobeyed their superiors and fraternized with "the enemy" along two-thirds of the Western Front (in times of war, a crime punishable by death). German troops held Christmas trees up out of the trenches with signs, "Merry Christmas," "You no shoot, we no shoot." Thousands of troops streamed across a no-man's land strewn with rotting corpses. They sang Christmas carols, exchanged photographs of loved ones back home, shared rations, played football, even roasted some pigs. Soldiers embraced men they had been trying to kill a few short hours before. They agreed to warn each other if the top brass forced them to fire their weapons, and to aim high.

A shudder ran through the high command on either side. Here was disaster in the making: soldiers declaring their brotherhood with each other and refusing to fight. Generals on both sides declared this spontaneous peacemaking to be treasonous and subject to court martial. By March 1915, the fraternization movement had been eradicated and the killing machine put back in full operation. By the time of the armistice in 1918, fifteen million would be slaughtered.

Even worse, the destruction wrought by World War I led directly to the rise of Hitler and Nazi Germany, the Communist Revolution and the Stalinist regime in Russia, the Holocaust that afflicted the Jews, and the horror of World War II.

Why do people do this to themselves?

Look at the deadly conflicts down through the ages;

Greece against the World
Rome against the World
Britain vs. Spain
Britain vs. France
Britain vs. the US
the US Civil War
World War I
World War II

To name a few.

Now look at the present-day membership of the European Union and of the Organisation for Economic Co-operation and Development (OECD), to name two of the better-known alliances.

Many of the countries that fought so bitterly in the past today are the closest of friends.

In 1943, Matthew Halton reported on the bloody street combat that claimed so many Canadian and German lives over Christmas 1943 in Ortona, Italy. Over Christmas 1999, CBC reporter David Halton, Matthew's son, wrote the final epilogue to his father's reports. Interviewing the same soldiers his father followed, Halton was there as the Canadian and German veterans reconciled.

Said Canadian veteran Ted Griffiths at the time: "This meeting has been a cleansing of the soul in many ways. It's a shedding of some of the ghosts of Ortona. They have forgiven us sort of thing, we have forgiven them ... and we've come together in the spirit of friendship."

Many of you will know that the beautiful cathedral at Coventry, England, was destroyed during one terrible German air raid during the war.

Today, Coventry has taken it as its mission to be a symbol of reconciliation for the world.

There is a statue there by Josefina de Vasconcellos, who made it at the age of ninety. It was donated to the Coventry Cathedral by Richard Branson on the fiftieth anniversary of the end of World War II (1995). A replica of this statue was donated by the people of Coventry to the peace garden of Hiroshima.

I know people who, sixty-five years ago, tried their very best to kill each other. Today, they like nothing better than to chat together over a beer about the World Cup of Soccer.

Many of them immigrated to Canada, which is how I came to know some of them. Their children and grandchildren have married each other and raised families.

So why did we fight? Why do people fight today when history tells us our motivations for killing each other will not be understood by our children and grandchildren?

Jean Vanier, the founder of l'Arche, has said: "Love has a transforming power. It is first and foremost a revelation of a person's essential, fundamental beauty and value. If nobody reveals to children their innate beauty and value, they will never know the importance and meaning of their life. They will hide behind sulking, depression, violence, aggressive attitudes or will try to prove their brilliance. When they are listened to and loved, they begin to discover what it means to be human. Little by little they become more trusting and want to live more fully. They realise they do not have to defend or prove themselves or always be at the centre of the stage; they have a place, they belong."

In this respect, nations are like children. If you treat them with love and respect, they will love and respect you.

If you bomb them and kill them, they will bomb and kill you.

And it needs to be said: they will not see bombs and missiles as signs of love and caring.

L'Arche began in 1964, when Jean Vanier and Father Thomas Philippe, in response to a call from God, invited Raphaël Simi and Philippe Seux, two men with mental handicaps, to come and share their life in the spirit of the Gospel and the Beatitudes that Jesus preached.

From this first community, born in France and in the Roman Catholic tradition, many other communities have developed in various cultural and religious traditions.

These communities, called into being by God, are united by the same vision and the same spirit of welcome, of sharing and simplicity.

Wikipedia, the internet encyclopaedia, lists the following as two of the fundamental principles of l'Arche:

1. Whatever their gifts or their limitations, people are all bound together in a common humanity. Everyone is of unique and sacred value, and everyone has the same dignity and the same rights. The fundamental rights of each person include the right to life, to care, to a home, to education and to work. Also, since the deepest need of a human being is to love and to be loved, each person has a right to friendship, to communion, and to a spiritual life.

2. If human beings are to develop their abilities and talents to the full, realizing all their potential as individuals, they need an environment that fosters personal growth. They need to form relationships with

others within families and communities. They need to live in an atmosphere of trust, security and mutual affection. They need to be valued, accepted and supported in real and warm relationships.

Surely these are also fundamental principles of humanity?

Micah told us that God required us only "to do justice, and to love kindness, and to walk humbly with your God."

Jesus told us he came that we might have life and have it more abundantly.

Jesus considered us as all worth saving. He said, "I have other sheep that do not belong to this fold. I must bring them also, and they will listen to my voice. So, there will be one flock, one shepherd."

And Jesus said, "Come to me, **all you that are weary** and are carrying heavy burdens, and I will give you rest. Take my yoke upon you, and learn from me; for I am gentle and humble in heart, and you will find rest for your souls." (emphasis added)

He wasn't just talking to the righteous ones among us who were weary. He was talking to all of us. Jesus was talking about love.

Several weeks ago, Neville gave a wonderful reflection that resonated with me. He said that he was not so much concerned with Christology and theology and all the other "ologies" as he was with friendship.

I could not agree more. And I would add to that love. Active love. Love where we give until it hurts.

Love where we spend our time, our treasure, and our talents

- on famine relief,

- on the marginalized,

- on medicines and medical help for AIDS and all other diseases and afflictions,

- on rebuilding homes destroyed by earthquakes and war.

And not

- on bombs,

- on missiles and tanks,

- on land mines, and

- on nuclear weapons.

Love where we spend our national treasure on construction, not destruction.

Love where we treat our neighbours as we would want them to treat us if we were them and they were us.

And then, "the lion and the lamb shall lie down together and every man, woman and child shall sit under their own vine and fig tree and none shall be afraid."

Amen

CHAPTER 14

In 2008, I was toying with the idea of becoming a professional speaker. This was one of the speeches I developed for the purpose. This one was presented to a meeting of a Kiwanis Club in my hometown of Scarborough, Ontario.

FIVE SECRETS TO MAKING A GREAT SPEECH (2008)

Skiing

When I was nine, my mum and dad bought my brothers and me skis, boots, and poles and took us skiing.

Now, understand, I love my mum and dad. However, for the life of me, I cannot fathom what they thought would happen when they took a nine-year-old klutz to a ski hill, put him on skis, and told him to have fun.

Without the benefit of lessons, I was expected to get myself to the top of the hill, and then back to the bottom, without killing myself or anyone else.

Fortunately, time has blotted out the painful memory of how I managed to use a rope tow or a pommel lift to get up the hill.

But I still remember in excruciating detail how I got down. I was scared to death of killing myself. I would pick the smallest, widest hill with a large, flat area at the bottom.

Then I would sit on the back of my skis—yes, that's right, sit on the back of my skis—and slide partway down the hill.

I was only nine. I knew nothing about aerodynamics! I didn't know that would just make me go faster!

When I was going so fast that I was getting scared, I would crash. That was the only way I knew how to stop.

Then I would pick myself up and point myself down the hill again. I would let myself go and slide straight down the hill and pray nobody got in my way. If somebody did, I would crash, usually before I hit them, then pick myself up, sit on my skis again, and repoint myself down the hill.

If nobody got in my way, and if God answered my prayers, I would finally get to the bottom in one piece and slide until I stopped.

For the next sixteen years, that was how I skied! Each year I would go skiing once or twice. Each year, I would get down the hill in the same proven way. For years I didn't have the energy or vision to figure out what I was doing that was wrong.

They say one definition of insanity is doing the same thing over and over again and expecting a different result!

Somehow, I never broke a leg or an arm, be it mine or anyone else's. But it did seem grossly unfair to me that I would pay the same price for lift tickets as everyone else and I would go up and down a hill three times a day while they would go up and down thirty times.

That all changed when I was twenty-five. I took lessons!

Within a week or two of starting my lessons, I had learned important secrets of how to ski. I learned how to snow plow, how to Stem Christie, and how to parallel turn.

All of a sudden, I was making fewer mistakes and actually having fun. And my cost per descent decreased by 90 per cent! Why, I wondered, hadn't I taken lessons sixteen years earlier? Think of the pain I could have avoided and the fun I could have had!

The Purpose of My Talk Today

Secrets to success are not limited to skiing. They exist in every endeavour we choose to pursue; for example, golf, home renovations, and, yes, making speeches!

Over the years, I have heard many great speakers, either in person or on film, on tape or in print. I have also heard or read what many of these same great speakers have said were the secrets to making a great speech.

The purpose of my talk to you today is to share with you what people down through the ages have learned about what makes a great public speaker.

Just as there are secrets you can learn to help you have more fun skiing, there are secrets you can learn to help you have more fun the next time you have to speak at a wedding or a Kiwanis Club meeting.

Outline

So what I am going to share with you today are five secrets that great speakers know about making memorable speeches.

Secret # 1: Speak with Enthusiasm!

Great speakers only talk about topics they really care about.

In 1971, I was looking forward to graduating from Western's School of Business with my MBA. I had majored in marketing. One of the interviews I went to was with F. H. Hayhurst, an ad agency, now part of Saatchi and Saatchi.

The interviewer was Jim Hayhurst Sr. He was young, about thirty, good looking, and personable. I liked him.

He welcomed me and asked me if I smoked. I said yes, but that I was trying to quit.

He asked me what I thought of cigarettes. I said I thought they caused lung cancer, emphysema, and heart disease and killed people before their time.

He asked me if I knew that Hayhurst had the Rothman's account. (You might recall that Rothman's used to be a popular brand of cigarettes).

- I said no, I did not.

He asked me if I would work on the Rothman's account.

- I said no, I would not.

He asked me if I knew that Hayhurst had profit-sharing.

- I said no, I did not.

He said under their profit-sharing plan, the profits from the Rothman's account were shared with all employees. Would I, he asked, accept profits from the Rothman's account?

- I said, thank you very much for your time!

The whole interview took about three minutes. It had a powerful impact on me.

It taught me to learn a bit more about the companies I was interviewing before I met with them.

More importantly, it made the point to me that it was important that I

1. knew what my values were, and

2. made sure I worked for a company that shared those values.

I left that interview with profound respect for Mr. Hayhurst. He had saved me from a move that would have been wrong for me and wrong for his company. I know I would not have been motivated to sell cigarettes! Obviously, he did too!!

It's exactly the same in public speaking. Enthusiasm is contagious. Whatever the topic, if you care passionately about your subject, your audience will too. But if you don't, they won't!

Secret # 2: Be Yourself

Relax and be yourself. That's what the audience wants.

Look at Elvis Presley. He has spawned thousands of imitators, undoubtedly some of whom were better entertainers than he was. But nobody remembers their versions of "Heartbreak Hotel."

Did you know the Beatles started their career by covering Elvis's hits? Do you remember any of their recordings of "Blue Suede Shoes"?

The bad news?

- You are not Winston Churchill.

- You are not Martin Luther King Jr.

- You are not Princess Di.

The good news? Nobody expects you to be!

What worked for them might not work for you. It is **your** personality that will make your talk come alive. Make sure that the language and style you use works for you. If it doesn't feel right to you, change it.

As Shakespeare's Polonius said to his son Laertes, "This above all, to thine own self be true, and it must follow as the night the day, thou canst not then be false to any man."

I played Polonius in a Grade 12 production of *Hamlet*. I will never forget those wonderful lines. You can only be a second best somebody else. Be the best that you can be.

Secret # 3: Tell Personal Stories

David Brooks, the 1990 World Champion of Public Speaking, quotes renowned public speaker Bill Gove as saying that the secret to public speaking is simply this:

- Make a point, tell a story.

- Make another point, tell another story.

- Make yet another point, tell yet another story.

That's all there is to it, he said.

Numbers have their place in presentations, especially in business presentations. But … people just are not as interested in statistics, no matter how impressive, as they are in real life stories about real people. And the best stories are your stories about your own personal experiences.

Some years ago, I had the pleasure of listening to a group of volunteers who were to represent the United Way on a speakers' bureau. These people had no experience in public speaking. They were extremely shy and very self-deprecating about their abilities to speak in public. All they had going for them was that they all had been helped by member agencies of the United Way.

They sold themselves short! Their personal stories were gut-wrenchingly powerful. Truth and emotion will trump glibness every time out.

Stories have the added advantage of being easy for you, the presenter, to remember, as well as being easy for the audience to remember.

And if they remember your story, they remember the point the story is intended to illustrate.

Secret # 4: Put Your Body and Soul into Your Speech

- *A speech is more than words*

According to a classic study by Dr. Albert Mehrabian of UCLA in 1971, an audience "listens" to and judges the "emotional content" of a speech based on the three "Vs":

- Visual (body language) 55 per cent.

- Vocal (how you sound) 38 per cent.

- Verbal (content) 7 per cent.

That doesn't work if your content is nonsense! But it makes the point that content alone is not enough!

If your content is sound but you deliver your speech with no body language in a flat monotone, you will put everyone to sleep.

It is so important to deliver your speech dynamically. Make eye contact with the audience, use your hands to make points—think conversation, not lecture. Vary your tone and cadence, emphasis and enthusiasm. Pause.

- *Exercise! Breathe!*

To settle the adrenaline down before you go on, it is sometimes helpful to go for a quick walk or to do some other physical routine. Alternatively, you might try taking a deep breath and letting it out slowly five or ten times.

Using gestures that involve large muscles during your speech is another way to allow the adrenaline pumping through your system to dissipate.

Secret # 5: Prepare. Prepare. Prepare.

The more prepared you are, the more relaxed you will be during your presentation. Nothing makes us more nervous than having unresolved issues outstanding as we are trying to speak.

Think about it.

- How relaxed can you be if you don't have a clear idea of what points you want to make and why?

- How relaxed can you be during your presentation if you arrive breathless and late at the venue?

- How relaxed can you be if you have not gone to the washroom in the last two hours and are wondering if your hair is askew or your skirt is straight?

Preparation is key. Know your audience. Know your topic. Plan your talk logically.

Know your location and its set-up. Get there ahead of time to get the lay of the land. Practise, or at least visually anticipate, your entry and exit. Do you run up the stairs to the stage? If using audio-visual aids, check to see that the hardware and software are compatible with your material (laptop, version of PowerPoint, etc.). If using a microphone on a stand, is it adjustable? If it is a lapel mic, where will you attach it? If using a tele-prompter, can you rehearse ahead of time?

Rehearse by saying the speech out loud—ideally in front of a group of friends. They can tell you if the speech is working well. There is no better place to practise your public speaking than at your local Toastmasters Club. Find one at www.toastmasters.org. There are over 11,000 clubs around the world and one of them is near you.

But if you don't have time for a full-dress rehearsal, saying the speech out loud to yourself helps to identify the language, flow, and turns of phrase that look fine when written but don't work when spoken.

Recap

So let me recap the five secrets to making a speech that all great speakers know.

1. Speak with enthusiasm.

2. Be yourself.

3. Tell personal stories.

4. Put your body and soul into your speech.

5. Prepare. Prepare. Prepare.

In 2007, thirty-six years after my fateful interview with Jim Hayhurst, I got in touch with him and shared with him an earlier draft of this speech. He is now a motivational speaker himself and told me he agreed with my points. And he told me the following story.

When his son Jimmy was twelve years old, he was in the district finals for his school's public speaking contest. In his speech, he spoke about that iconic Canadian painting school, the Group of Seven. Jimmy's grandfather was a fan of the Group of Seven, and Jimmy had spent many hours talking to his grandfather about them. He felt he was an expert.

In the district finals, however, Jimmy lost to a boy who talked about the contents of his school locker!

Jimmy was furious. He collared one of the judges and gave him what for. How could he, Jimmy said, give the prize to a boy talking about something so mundane as his locker, when Jimmy was talking about something truly important, like the Group of Seven?

The judge kindly and patiently explained to Jimmy that the other boy knew more about the contents of his locker than Jimmy knew about the Group of Seven. And he spoke about them with more enthusiasm and excitement than Jimmy spoke about the Group of Seven.

It was a lesson that Jimmy and his father never forgot. For a speech to be great it must be delivered with enthusiasm, by someone intimately connected with the story being told.

Go and do likewise!

Mr. Chair

CHAPTER 15

An address I made to the Speakers Toastmasters Club on the occasion of their thirtieth anniversary.

THE GOOD OLD DAYS—TAKE 1— DECEMBER 15, 2008

Why are you in Toastmasters?

(Take responses from the audience.)

In my case, there were several other reasons. I originally joined a French-language club in Quebec because I wanted to improve my French. I think many people join Toastmasters to improve either their English or their Canadian accent.

In 1972, I joined Scarborough Toastmasters for three main reasons:

1. To keep my brain alive without having to take night school courses with their attendant exams.

2. To socialize with my brother, Stan, who was a member of Scarborough.

3. As a social thing. I was single in the big city and it was something to do.

But whatever our other reasons might be, I think we all share one reason: we want to become better public speakers.

OK. So that's why you joined. You become a better public speaker. Your English/French/whatever improves. You make friends.

Why do you stay?

(Take responses from the audience)

I can only talk about my situation:

1. To keep my brain alive.

2. Because of the positive reinforcement. I gradually became a better speaker. I started feeling better about myself, more confident that I could handle situations, be they speaking situations or leadership situations.

3. Because of the friendships. Many of my best friends were fellow members of Scarborough Toastmasters.

So I went to club meetings knowing that at a minimum I would have an interesting club meeting and at a maximum I would also get to hang out with my friends. And it became a tightly interwoven family group.

One of my friends, Paul Bentley, was a teacher at Winston Churchill Collegiate Institute. And I am sure he was an excellent teacher.

But being a teacher in a classroom setting in front of a group of teenagers is different from speaking to a group of adults in a private room in a restaurant, which is where Scarborough met at that time.

I remember the first Table Topic Paul did. He stood up for ten seconds, looking like the proverbial deer caught in the headlights and said, "I'm sorry, I can't do this." And sat down.

He went on to become probably the finest speaker in the club. I particularly remember a speech he did on how to catch wasps in a marmalade jar. Amazing Essex accent, which he normally avoided. Thick. Wonderful.

Paul became a backbone of Scarborough and a strong member of its executive.

That was Scarborough Toastmasters Club in 1978.

A tightly knit group of friends. An excellent club. Ran like clockwork.

Those were the good old days.

But we had a problem.

Time marches inexorably on. TI only allowed forty members in a club, and we had forty-three. What to do? Refuse new members? Split up?

After much soul-searching, it was decided the responsible thing to do was to split. I and just over half the membership would continue on as Scarborough Toastmasters. Paul, our VP of education, and the rest of the membership would leave to form a brand-new club, Speakers Toastmasters Club, under Paul's leadership as the founding president.

Some people, like my brother Stan here, joined both clubs.

Frankly, I found the start of Speakers to be a real strain.

At the time, Scarborough had about forty-three members. Let's call them A to Z and one to seventeen. Let's assume that of those members, one, N, was really good friends with A, B, C, and D. B was also a good friend of E, F, and G. C was a good friend of H, I, and J. Etcetera. You get the picture.

When we formed Speakers, Paul, let's call him A, took B through M and one through eight with him. And letters N through Z and nine through seventeen were left behind. The Toastmasters family was split in half. It was very traumatic.

Meanwhile, my personal family situation had also evolved.

Single when I joined, the same month that Speakers was formed, my wife and I had our third child, Jennifer. Sixteen months later, much to our surprise, our fourth child, Doug, was born. Evenings at a nice dinner with my Toastmaster friends were a luxury that, time-wise, I could no longer afford.

I quit Toastmasters. The good old days of Scarborough and Toastmasters were gone.

For the next eight years I concentrated on my family and my career.

As rewarding and challenging as those were, I found I missed the friendships and mental stimulation and confidence-building of Toastmasters. And my speaking abilities were becoming rusty.

I decided to come back to Toastmasters. I still could not reconcile my schedule to Scarborough's, but I did find another club that met at a time and place that better suited my schedule.

And that showed me one of the wonderful benefits of this brotherhood and sisterhood we call Toastmasters, because I have restored friendships with Toastmasters that I met when I first joined Scarborough.

The good times that I had in Scarborough are now an all-too-distant memory. But the good times I am having at Bay Street Breakfast, at Toastmasters conferences and working with people like Jyl McGunigal, and indeed being here at Speakers this evening, are very much alive.

So congratulations to Speakers on still being here, thirty years on. Congratulations to you all, whether you have been members for one month, one year, or whatever period of time.

And enjoy every minute you are together, because, trust me, **these are the good old days!**

Madam Toastmaster!

CHAPTER 16

EULOGY FOR DAD—JANUARY 2009

PECK, Robert Cartwright

After a lengthy battle, courageously borne, Bob died peacefully at home on Saturday, January 10, 2009. Beloved husband of Margery (née Upton) for sixty-five years. Wonderful father to Stan (Mary), Rob (Julia), Bruce, Weston (Cathy), and the late infant Janet. Grandpa of Michael, Gordon, David, Ross, Jennifer, Douglas (Jessica), Graham, and Linda. He is survived by his brother George (late wife Mary) and many nieces and nephews. Bob was a long-time employee of Alcan, working in British Guiana; Geneva, Switzerland; Newport, England; Shawinigan Falls, Quebec; Copenhagen, Denmark; and Toronto, Kingston, and Etobicoke, Ontario; retiring in 1973 from Birmingham, England, after thirty-two years' service. Bob and Margery moved to Peterborough after retirement, where they have lived happily for the last thirty-five years. Visitation will be held from 7–9 p.m. on Thursday, January 15, at **COMSTOCK FUNERAL HOME & CREMATION**

These were my remarks at my dad's memorial service in January 2009.

Hi. My name is Rob Peck. Bob Peck was my dad.

My son Doug tells me a good model for church reflections is the following: challenge in the world, grace in the world. Start with the challenge, end with the grace.

That really works for me. So I am going to talk about Dad's travel, medical issues, work, and family life.

First, the challenge, then the grace.

Travel

Dad met Mum at the University of Alberta in Edmonton, where he studied civil engineering and she studied home ec. After graduation in 1940, Dad went to work for the Aluminum Company of Canada in British Guiana (aka BG).

In March of 1943, Mum arrived in BG, and very soon after they were married.

Between 1943 and 1973, Mum and Dad moved ten times, for an average of once every three years. From BG to Ontario, back to BG, to Switzerland, to England, to Quebec, back to Ontario, to Denmark, back to England, and, finally, back to Canada.

In the course of those moves, they picked up five kids: Stan in 1944, me in '46, Bruce in '48, Weston in '51, and Janet in '61. Tragically, Janet died as a small baby.

Amidst the challenge of always roaming, forever making and leaving new friends, the church was a grounding presence ... Mum and Dad had one rule: find a church and join the choir. In Canada, it was the United Church... Elsewhere, it might be Methodist, Lutheran, or Anglican. Within six months of arriving in a new town, they would be totally plugged into their church community.

And living in foreign countries was not all hardship. Switzerland, Denmark, and England are not hardship posts!

While in Europe, they took advantage of the opportunity to travel extensively and learn new languages. And they made many friends with whom they still keep in touch.

But Mum told Dad on his retirement that she wanted to find a nice place where they could stay and where they wouldn't have to leave their friends.

They chose Peterborough for several reasons. It reminded them of Calgary, it had a university, and it wasn't too close to the kids.

One of the first things they did was find Trinity United Church—where they found a good community …

God's community.

The travels continued but now were in the form of vacations. Thirty-two years of moves and dislocations were followed by thirty-five years of grace in Peterborough.

Medical

Bob had a number of life-threatening medical challenges. Some examples include tuberculosis, a collapsed lung, a ruptured gall bladder, a serious stroke, and several different types of cancers.

Our son Doug remembers swimming in Grandma and Grandpa's pool, seeing Grandpa in his swimsuit, and noticing he had many more belly buttons than the average man.

When Doug asked him about it, Grandpa told him about his many surgeries in a very concise, matter-of-fact manner. Dad could laugh at the hand he was dealt. He took it all in stride and continued living his life right up to the end.

During the past few days, Mum has often said we were fortunate to have him for sixty-five years, about thirty years more than Dad and his brother George had their dad.

Comes to that, Dad always used to say his goal was to make it to the year 2000. And he did do that! In large part due to Mum's love and support. Mum is incredibly strong mentally, emotionally, and physically. While she has had some medical challenges of her own, she has never let them get in the way of looking after Dad. We think she is the reason he made it so far against such long odds.

Work and Family Life

Several years ago, I asked him, "Dad, you had so many good jobs, manager of this, director of that. What job did you like the most?"

He thought for only a few seconds and said, "None of them."

It then occurred to me that during his working years, Dad had been under more stress than I had ever realized. Because he never brought it home to us, we never knew.

Dad was always willing to listen to us when we had a problem. Mind you, don't ever think our house was a democracy. There was never any question of that. Mum and Dad were fond of saying it was a benevolent dictatorship!

Mum and Dad's support was unconditional. They would often say, "Just remember that no matter what happens, we love you and we are proud of you." That was always a great comfort to me.

Some years ago, I asked Dad at what age he stopped worrying about us. He said, "When I get there, I'll let you know."

We are so grateful for the positive example that Mum and Dad set for us of a loving relationship, a strong family unit, and encouragement to do your best.

We only hope that the superb example they have set for us, and that we have tried to emulate, will give our children the same strong, confident start in life that Mum and Dad gave us.

CHAPTER 17

A speech I gave to a Toastmasters' district officers' training function in 2009.

WHY OFFICERS' TRAINING?

Skiing

When I was nine, my mum and dad bought my brothers and me skis, boots, and poles, and took us skiing.

Now understand, I love my mum and dad. However, for the life of me, I cannot fathom what they thought would happen when they took a nine-year-old klutz to a ski hill, put him on skis, and told him to have fun.

Without the benefit of lessons, I was expected to get myself to the top of the hill, and then back to the bottom, without killing myself or anyone else.

Fortunately, time has blotted out the painful memory of how I managed to use a rope tow or a pommel lift to get up the hill.

But I still remember in excruciating detail how I got down. I was scared to death of killing myself. I would pick the smallest, widest hill with a large, flat area at the bottom.

Then I would sit on the back of my skis—yes, that's right, sit on the back of my skis—and slide about halfway down the hill.

Then I would crash. That was the only way I knew how to stop.

Then I would pick myself up and point myself down the hill. I would let myself go and slide straight down the hill and pray nobody got in my way. If somebody did, I would crash again, usually before I hit them, then pick myself up, sit on my skis again, and repoint myself down the hill.

If nobody got in my way, and if God answered my prayers, I would finally get to the bottom in one piece and slide until I stopped.

For the next sixteen years, that was how I skied! Each year I would go skiing once or twice. Each year I would get down the hill in the same proven way. For years, I didn't have the energy or vision to figure out what I was doing that was wrong.

Somehow, I never broke a leg or an arm—mine or anyone else's. But it did seem grossly unfair to me that I would pay the same price for lift tickets as everyone else, and I would go up and down a hill three times a day while they would go up and down thirty times.

That all changed when I was twenty-five. I took lessons! Within a week or two of starting my lessons, I learned how to snow plow, how to Stem Christie, and how to parallel turn. All of a sudden, I was making fewer mistakes and actually having fun. And my cost per descent decreased by 90 per cent! Why, I wondered, hadn't I taken lessons sixteen years earlier? Think of the pain I could have avoided and the fun I could have had!

Officers' Training

The advantages of training are not limited to skiing. They exist in every endeavour we choose to pursue—for example, golf, home renovations, and, yes, Toastmasters!

The purpose of my talk to you today is to tell you something of what I have learned about why officers' training is of paramount importance to the health and wellbeing of Toastmasters and the clubs they belong to. Just as skiing lessons helped me have more fun skiing, officers' training can help you avoid the pain of needless mistakes and to have more fun performing your role on your club's executive.

There are three ways to learn about how to run a Toastmasters club well:

Method Number 1: Join the perfect club where everything is always done perfectly.

I have come close to Method # 1. I was a member of Scarborough Toastmasters Club from 1972 to 1979. Under the able mentorship of Jim Dearness and Jim Rollingson, long-time members of the club who had exceedingly high standards, the club flourished.

For reasons that are the subject of another speech, I had to quit Toastmasters, and Scarborough, in 1979. When I came back in 1987, I joined Toronto Downtown Toastmasters Club. Another great club, run really well by a group of Toastmasters with, again, high standards.

With those clubs as examples, I and others, started Bay Street Breakfast Toastmasters Club in 1991. Bay Street has been blessed in the ensuing years with many Toastmasters of exceptional ability who care enough to insist on maintaining high standards.

But while I would be the first to say those three clubs all had remarkable Toastmasters who strove to achieve and maintain high standards, I would be the last to say they were perfect. Each was and is run by human beings with human failings.

So if Scarborough, Toronto Downtown, and Bay Street Breakfast are not perfect, how is one to find the perfect club?

Let me know if you figure it out. Me? I am still looking!

Method Number 2: Make Every Mistake in the Book.

The problem with this method was the same one I faced with my skiing. There are not enough hours in one lifetime for anyone, no matter how brilliant, to figure out what all of humankind has taken thousands of years to figure out.

Even Isaac Newton admitted he only accomplished what he did because he had stood on the shoulders of giants!

Which brings us to Method Number 3: Go to officers' training, where people who have learned the hard way will tell you what they wish they had done differently.

When I first joined Toastmasters, I was not aware, in any real sense, of anything outside of my individual club.

Officers' training raises your eyes above the horizon of your individual club (great as it may be!), to the world beyond.

Toastmasters has been in existence since 1924. Millions of people have been members. Over 200,000 people today are members of over 11,000 clubs in over ninety countries around the world.

Do you know what that means? That means that every problem you have ever had in Toastmasters, or ever will have, someone else has already had and solved!

You can save untold time and heartache by simply learning from those who have already made the mistakes you are about to make! You don't need to fall into the same traps they did!

And avoiding problems before they occur is less work than fixing them afterward.

Trust me! Everything is a lot more fun if you know what you are doing!

And there is a bonus reason for going to officers' training—to meet other dedicated Toastmasters.

Officers' training shows you that you are not alone. There are people out there who care about you and your problems and stand ready to help.

It has been said that there are three kinds of people in the world:

a. people who are in the parade,

b. people who are watching the parade, and

c. people who don't even know there is a parade!

By virtue of your being here, you have shown yourselves to be people who want to be in the parade.

You are my kind of people! I like people who want to have a positive impact on their environment. I find it is more fun to go through life surrounded by upbeat, positive doers than people who sit back and hope life comes to them.

And one of the major benefits of officers' training is that you meet many people like yourself who, coincidentally, can help you out of problems you don't even know you are going to have! So when that unexpected problem does occur, you have names, phone numbers, and e-mail addresses of people who can help you out!

And, of course, helping is a two-way street. There is nothing more rewarding than knowing that you have helped a fellow Toastmaster by sharing with him or her your hard-earned lessons of what works and what doesn't.

Recap

So to recap: There are three ways to learn how to run your club better:

1. Join the perfect club. Problem? It is hard to find it.

2. Trial and error. Problem? There aren't enough lifetimes to make every mistake in the book and learn from them.

3. Go to officers' training, where other people will share their painfully learned secrets. And, as a bonus, you will make the greatest, neatest friends in the world!

So congratulations on being here! It was not only a kind and worthwhile decision that will benefit all of the members of your Club. It was a smart move that will save you a lot of wasted time spinning your wheels and will make you wonderful friends in the process!

Now ... what if you have heard everything I have said, but you don't buy it?

What if you don't take full advantage of officers' training? What if you blunder ahead and make all of those mistakes that others have made before ... because you think you are different and you know better?

Well, in those moments, I want you to remember that we Toastmasters have all been there. We all know how it feels. We all feel your pain!

And if and when you change your mind, we will be there for you! At the next officers' training!

Mr. Toastmaster!

CHAPTER 18

A keynote speech I gave to a Toastmasters division awards presentation in September 2009.

THE MOST IMPORTANT THING IN LIFE

What do you think is the most important thing in life?

Many people would say, "Love your neighbour as yourself." Most people in Canada know that commandment as the Golden Rule: Do unto others as you would have them do unto you! Did you know that the Golden Rule is in every major world religion and philosophy?

For example:

- **Buddhism:**

    - *Hurt not others in ways that you yourself would find hurtful."* Udana-Varga 5:18

- **Christianity:**

    - *"And as ye would that men should do to you, do ye also to them likewise."* Luke 6:31, King James Version.

- **Confucianism:**

  - *"Do not do to others what you do not want them to do to you."* Analects 15:23

- **Hinduism:**

  - *"This is the sum of duty: do not do to others what would cause pain if done to you."* Mahabharata 5:1517

- **Islam:**

  - *"None of you [truly] believes until he wishes for his brother what he wishes for himself."* Number 13 of Imam *"Al-Nawawi's Forty Hadiths."* ₅

- **Judaism:**

  - *"... thou shalt love thy neighbor as thyself."* Leviticus 19:18

- **Taoism:**

  - *"Regard your neighbor's gain as your own gain, and your neighbor's loss as your own loss."* T'ai Shang Kan Ying P'ien.

Now, implicit in the Golden Rule is that we must learn to love ourselves before we can love others. After all, if somebody inherently hates themselves, you would not want them to treat you the same way they treat themselves now, would you?

So for the Golden Rule to work, we must love ourselves first.

Otherwise stated, we must have self-respect!

As Polonius said to his son Laertes in Shakespeare's *Hamlet*:

"This above all: to thine own self be true, And it must follow, as the night the day, thou cans't not then be false to any man."

I played Polonius in a high-school production of *Hamlet*, and those words have been **indelibly** inscribed on my brain.

Self-respect. *That* is what I consider the most important thing in life. With self-respect, everything is possible. Without self-respect, it all gets a lot harder.

So if that is the most important thing, how do you get it?

I like what Whitney Griswold, the noted American historian and educator, said:

"Self-respect cannot be hunted. It cannot be purchased. It is never for sale. It cannot be fabricated out of public relations. It comes to us when we are alone, in quiet moments, in quiet places, when we suddenly realize that, knowing the good, we have done it; knowing the beautiful, we have served it; knowing the truth we have spoken it."

Think about those words. They are amongst the most insightful I have ever heard.

Now think about the good things *you* have done. The many hours you have spent with your children or other family members, helping them with their challenges. The organizations you volunteer for. The work you do for a living. Think about Toastmasters! The people in this room that you have helped to become better speakers and better leaders and, hence, better human beings.

Knowing the good, you have done it. Knowing the beautiful, you have served it. Knowing the truth, you have spoken it. And you have my respect!

Now it is true we don't *always* do the right thing. We have all fallen short of our own aspirations for ourselves at one time or another.

Robbie Burns said:

> "O wad some Pow'r the giftie gie us
> To see oursels as others see us
> It wad frae monie a blunder free us
> An' foolish notion."

Well, the giftie gie us Toastmasters!

And our Toastmasters friends, by shining a mirror back onto us, help to free us frae monie a blunder an' foolish notion!

Plan A is to do the right thing.

Plan B is to be truly sorry when we do the wrong thing, to try to make amends, and to forgive ourselves just as we forgive others when they hurt us.

So in summary:

Try to Do the good!
Try to Serve the beautiful!
Try to Speak the truth!

But do forgive yourself when you fall short,
just as you forgive others when they fall short.

Respect yourself.

Love yourself and love your fellow man.

And as the Jewish Talmud says, "What is hateful to you, do not to your fellow man. This is the law: all the rest is commentary."

Mr. Toastmaster

CHAPTER 19

In 2010 I was still toying with the idea of becoming a professional speaker. This was one speech I developed as part of my portfolio.

HOW TO BECOME A BETTER SPEAKER

I am happy to share with you some thoughts on how you can become a better speaker. These thoughts have developed over the last fifty years ... partly from personal experience and partly from observing others speak. I have been in Toastmasters for thirty of those fifty years.

These are the things I think are most important if you want to become a more effective public speaker.

Lesson #1:

1. **First, a story.**

   Jim Hayhurst, a motivational speaker, told me the following story.

   When his son Jimmy was twelve years old, he was in the district finals for his school's public speaking contest. In his speech he spoke about that iconic Canadian painting school, the Group of Seven. Jimmy's grandfather was a fan of the Group of Seven, and Jimmy had spent many hours talking to his grandfather about them. He felt he was an expert.

In the district finals, however, Jimmy lost to a boy who talked about the contents of his locker!

Jimmy was furious. He collared one of the judges and gave him what for. How could he, Jimmy said, give the prize to a boy talking about something so mundane as his locker, when Jimmy was talking about something truly important, like the Group of Seven?

The judge kindly and patiently explained to Jimmy that the other boy knew more about the contents of his locker than Jimmy knew about the Group of Seven. And he spoke about them with more enthusiasm and excitement than Jimmy spoke about the Group of Seven.

It was a lesson that Jimmy, and his father, never forgot. For a speech to be great, it must be delivered with enthusiasm, by someone intimately connected with the story being told.

So if you want to become a better speaker … Lesson #1:

Stick to topics you care about

Whatever you do in public speaking, it will only be effective if people really believe you mean it. Every time you speak, whether it is a prepared speech, an impromptu speech, acting as Toastmaster or evaluator—any role in any function—if it is worth doing at all, it must be done with conviction.

How do you feel when somebody introduces their remarks by comments such as:

> "I'm sorry, but I'm not really prepared to be general evaluator. I forgot all about it and haven't spoken to my evaluators yet," or

> "I just threw this together last night because …"

> "You probably won't agree with me. After all, what do I know? I don't really know very much about this topic."

Personally, if I hear comments like this, I discount the rest of what the speaker has to say. I am also frankly resentful that people have wasted my time telling me something they don't really believe in themselves.

So my tip is: Be in earnest. If you don't believe what you are saying, don't say it.

If you do believe it, throw your whole heart into it. Get emotional. Be there! And don't apologize.

If you could be better prepared, don't share that with us. That is your secret. We don't want to know.

Where can you speak just about any time you want, on any subject you want?

At Toastmasters!

So if you want to practise speaking on topics you care about,

Stay in Toastmasters!

2. **Another story**

One of the worst speeches I gave in my life was on whether the cottages on the Toronto Islands should be razed to allow the creation of more parkland. I researched it to death. I had statistics on statistics. Unfortunately, the islands were not a subject I felt passionately about. I tried to memorize the speech. The presentation was wooden. I lost my place. A major catastrophe. But it was worth it because it drove home an important lesson.

Unless you are an accomplished actor, memorized speeches tend to be wooden and flat. It takes so much effort to remember your exact words that your voice and your body language lose their vitality. Don't worry about getting your words exactly the way you wrote the speech in the first place. Just worry about getting the sense and spirit of what you wrote.

So Lesson #2

Lesson #2: Don't memorize

If spontaneity isn't everything, it verges on it. That hardly means winging it: careful preparation spawns spontaneity. But don't become a slave to detailed written notes. If you do, you become a slave to your exact wording and inevitably lose 75 per cent of any emotional impact.

Put your notes on index cards (written in large font) so that you won't be nailed to the lectern. Then wander—around the table, into the crowd, about the platform. Look comfortable and your audience will be more comfortable, too.

The other trick to doing speeches without detailed notes is important enough to be Lesson #3.

Lesson #3: Tell stories, stories, and more stories.

Charts and graphs have their place, and a pretty prominent one in business presentations. Nevertheless, as Tom Peters is fond of saying, even an analytically inclined audience will remember one poignant comment from a survey respondent ("This company really doesn't listen to the likes of us") long after forgetting your multi-coloured bar chart showing the firm's "openness to ideas" at 2.62 on a seven-point, socio-metrically valid scale.

The best speakers illustrate their talks with short, striking stories. In fact, the most powerful speeches are often little more than strings of such stories, loosely linked by some common theme.

And where can you hear stories, live stories, and practise telling stories?

At Toastmasters! So stay in Toastmasters!

Lesson #4: Loosen up, you're not going to convince them anyway.

Speeches aren't about turning arch-enemies into cheering supporters. Remember Martin Luther King Jr.'s "I have a dream" speech, given at the Lincoln Memorial on August 28, 1963?

You know the one. The most memorable lines were:

I have a dream
that one day
this nation will rise up
and live out the true meaning of its creed:
We hold these truths to be self-evident,
that all men are created equal.

I have a dream
that one day on the red hills of Georgia,
the sons of former slaves and the sons of former slave owners
will be able to sit down together at the table of brotherhood.

I have a dream
that my four little children
will one day live in a nation where they will not be judged by the colour
of their skin but by the content of their character.

I have a *dream* today!

That speech did not convert southern racists into champions of civil rights.

But it did lead to:

- In 1964 the Twenty-fourth Amendment to the U.S. constitution
  abolishing the poll tax and thus making it easier for poor Blacks
  to vote;

- Also in 1964, the Civil Rights Act of 1964, prohibiting dis-
  crimination of all kinds based on race, color, religion, or national
  origin; and,

- In 1965 the Voting Rights Act of 1965, abolishing literacy tests,
  poll taxes, and other such requirements that had been used in many
  southern states to make it difficult for Blacks to vote.

It inspired generations of Americans—Black, red, yellow, and white—to fight for their dreams. And on November 4, 2008, a Black American, Barack Obama, was elected president of the United States of America.

Speeches are mainly opportunities to reassure those who already agree with you that you're a horse worth betting on. So try to relax and enjoy yourself, to present "excited you" as excited you—which is just what the audience wants.

So to summarize

1. Stick to topics you care about.

2. Don't memorize.

3. Tell stories.

4. Loosen up.

And above all,

Stay in Toastmasters!

CHAPTER 20

WHAT MAKES A GREAT SPEECH—TAKE 2

In 2010, I put together my own list of the best attributes of great speeches.

I have tweaked it in subsequent years. While it summarizes my views on public speaking, and those of speakers I admire, it is only one approach; many other approaches would be equally valid, but this works for me.

1. **Love your subject**

   Whatever you do in public speaking, it will only be effective if people really believe you mean it. Every time you present, any role in any function, if it is worth doing at all, you must speak with conviction. If you do not believe what you are saying, do not say it.

2. **Don't try to be somebody you're not**

   Unless you are an accomplished actor, you cannot convince people you are Barack Obama or Oprah Winfrey. They are originals. You are an original. Be yourself.

3. **Tell personal stories**

   People do not remember many facts and numbers. They do remember vivid stories, and if they remember the story, they remember the point. The best speakers illustrate their talks with short, striking stories. The most powerful speeches are often strings of such stories, linked by a common theme.

4. **Put your body and soul into your presentation**

Do not worry about gestures or vocal variety. If you throw yourself into your speech, your body will mirror your feelings and the gestures and vocal variety will naturally follow.

5. **Don't worry about being nervous**

Most presenters are nervous—it is OK! Nervousness gives your presentation its electricity.

6. **Prepare. Prepare. Prepare.**

The best antidote to excessive nervousness is preparation. Next best is to worry about helping the other guy—that takes your concern off yourself.

7. **Have structure**

Opening, body, and conclusion. Tell us where you want to go and why. Then tell us where we've been and where we should go from here.

8. **Relax!**

Think conversation, not oration. Speeches aren't about turning archenemies into cheering supporters. Speeches are mainly opportunities to reassure those who already agree with you that you're a horse worth betting on. So relax and enjoy yourself.

9. **Practice. Practice. Practice.**

Get training. Present. Get feedback. Repeat.

CHAPTER 21

A speech I made to the Bay Street Breakfast Toastmasters in March 2010.

I ALWAYS WANTED TO LIVE FOREVER

I always wanted to live forever.

So far, so good!

But the father of a friend of mine succumbed to lung cancer when I was in college. I'll call him Harry. Harry was a heavy smoker. The day he got his diagnosis, he went into a funk. He went into his bedroom, drew the curtains, and waited to die. For all intents and purposes, he died that day.

That had a big impact on me. And it made me start thinking about preventive maintenance and risk avoidance.

Today, I want to talk to you about the importance of preventive maintenance and risk avoidance in living a long and healthy life, and the limitations of such a regime.

Bodies are sophisticated pieces of equipment, not unlike ships.

Preventive maintenance:

- If a ship's engine is never serviced, it will eventually blow.

- If a ship's hull is never painted, it will eventually rust out.

And risk avoidance

- If you sail a ship into a hurricane, chances are it will sink!

What is good for a ship is good for us!

So, generally speaking, I have taken care of my body.

I practise preventive maintenance:

- I have regular check-ups.

- I go to the gym regularly … Heck, sometimes I even exercise!

And I practise risk avoidance. I quit smoking on January 20, 1972. Yes, I know the day. The day before my twenty-sixth birthday. Because I was told if you quit smoking when you are twenty-five, and survive to be thirty, your life expectancy will be the same as if you had never smoked at all.

Now I don't know if that is true, but it sure motivated me to quit! And I think it was a good decision, because I now am older than Harry was when he died of lung cancer.

Mind you, I still have my faults!

I drink too much Coke and too many Iced Capps. I like pie and cake and cookies and ice cream. Maybe one day all that sugar will catch up to me and I will contract diabetes!

But … I submit to you … preventive maintenance and risk avoidance are only half the story!

As William Shedd said, "A ship is safe in harbour, but that is **not** what ships are for."

How many of you have heard of Randy Pausch? Or the Last Lecture?

Randy Pausch was a professor of computer science at Carnegie Mellon University in Pittsburgh who died last year of pancreatic cancer.

Cancer killed Randy, but, unlike Harry, he didn't let it beat him. Before he died, he inspired millions of people with his Last Lecture. The last time I looked, it had over 11 million hits on YouTube. The moving and often humorous talk told of his efforts to achieve such childhood dreams as becoming a professional football player, experiencing zero gravity, and developing Disney World attractions. In the process, he shared his insights on finding the good in other people, working hard to overcome obstacles, and living generously. His message was about following your dreams, dealing with the ones that don't come true, and having fun along the way.

So what's my point?

Unfortunately, there are no guarantees in life. Your ship can be perfectly maintained and perfectly piloted, and you can still be sunk by a tsunami or other disaster.

You can do everything to be healthy and still be cut down by a dread disease or a drunk driver.

So *do* maintain your ship. Do not sail into hurricanes. But *do* sail your ship out of the harbour. Follow your dreams. Deal with the ones that don't come true. And have fun along the way.

Because, ladies and gentlemen, none of us is going to live forever.

Madam Toastmaster

CHAPTER 22

This speech was delivered in 2010 but was about a vacation Julia and I and our four children took in 1989.

TEN SLEEP CANYON

Twenty-one years ago, my family had a major family reunion in Creston, B.C. One week after that, my wife, Julia's, family had a wedding in Calgary. Just a day's drive east of Creston.

There was nothing for it. We had to go.

When I was a boy in 1959, our family drove out west through Canada and back through the US via Yellowstone National Park. It was a wonderful holiday that I have always treasured in my memory. Julia and I decided to reprise it. So after some research, we rented a twenty-seven-foot C-Class motor home for four weeks and headed west. This is the rig.

But to be different, we headed out via the US and came back through Canada. The first few days were fairly straightforward. Most of the terrain was flat. We coped with southwestern Ontario, Michigan, Illinois, Iowa, and South Dakota fairly well. Then we hit Wyoming and the Bighorn Mountains. Not a big mountain range. Actually, a junky mountain range. Old, weathered, and worn down. We stopped at a tourist information office to ask which route we should take to get across the Bighorn Mountains to Yellowstone National Park.

"Do you want to take the scenic route or the boring route?" they asked. "The scenic route is more challenging."

Understand we had only been driving this big twenty-seven-foot motor home for less than a week. "Boring, I said. "We like boring!"

"Take US16," they said, "through the Ten Sleep Canyon."

So we headed out along US16. Everything was flat as far as the eye could see.

Or I thought it was flat. Julia was the first one to twig to the fact that we were going uphill.

"Look, Rob", she said, "at the ditches. The water in the ditches." Sure enough, the water was running the other way in the ditches!

"What goes up must come down, Rob," Julia said. "Sooner or later, we are going to have to pay for this!"

Then we saw the sign. "Seven to eight percent grade for the next twenty-seven miles. Trucks, check your brakes." We had only just rented the RV the week before. We had no idea what the brakes were like! Hopefully, they were OK!

So, with trepidation, we continued.

Suddenly, the full horror of our situation became apparent. Lying ahead of us was a mini–Grand Canyon. A two or three mile wide, and apparently twenty-seven-mile-long gouge taken out of the land. When we came, it was invisible, disappearing into the landscape. But now we were upon it.

The road went over the edge and along the side of a straight drop to the canyon floor two thousand feet below.

The road was two lanes wide. It was paved. I will give you that. But it had no shoulders to speak of. And no guard rails. Not even posts. If you drove off the road, it was clear sailing until you smashed into the ground two thousand feet below.

That was the bad news.

The good news was that we were on the canyon wall side. We had a whole lane of road between us and oblivion! Julia put the truck into first gear and, riding the brakes, we gingerly went down the hill.

Then our worst fears were realized. A switchback! We had to turn 180 degrees. That was bad enough. And at least they had about ten posts in the ground at the turn. No cables tying them together, though. And the RV's centre of gravity was so high that it would have toppled right over any posts anyway.

But the worst part was now we were on the outside. No lane of road, no shoulder, nothing between us and eternity! And I was in the passenger seat, just feet from the edge. Not that I wanted to drive! No way. If we were going to die, it was not going to be my fault!

Just to make sure we fully appreciated the gravity (get that? gravity!) of our situation, every kilometre or so, white crosses appeared on the side of the highway, presumably indicating where some poor soul went over the edge.

Well, our trip down that canyon wall seemed to go on forever. As quickly as we descended, the canyon descended just as quickly. Always the drop seemed to stay at two thousand feet. But finally, finally, after about half an hour, we got down to the canyon floor. Against all the odds, we had survived.

"Julia," I said, "you have just passed mountain driving 101! But God help us, we still have the Rockies ahead of us. And they are *real* mountains!"

Her reply was, "If that was mountain driving 101, then put me on a plane and send me home!" You need to know that Julia hates flying.

We have been out west, since.

But we flew!

Mr. Toastmaster

CHAPTER 23

This was a presentation I gave on September 23, 2010, to the 1,001st meeting of the Bay Street Breakfast Club, celebrating 1,000 meetings of BSBC.

"AHA!" MOMENTS

"Aha!" moments. We have all had them. Those joyous moments, unique and special to each of us, when the relationship between two or more distinct points suddenly becomes clear in our mind.

This evening, I would like to share with you three "Aha!" moments in my life. Funnily enough, they all relate to Toastmasters!

"Aha!" Moment #1. Since the best speeches are Ice Breakers, we should strive to make every speech an Ice Breaker.

First, you need to know what an Ice Breaker speech is.

For the non-Toastmasters in the crowd, the Ice Breaker is the first formal prepared speech performed by a new Toastmaster. To make the new Toastmaster as comfortable as possible in this nerve-wracking experience, the Ice Breaker's subject is the person him or herself. The thought is:

1. if you really know your subject, you will be more relaxed and

2. the subject we all know best is ourselves, so we should tell stories about ourselves.

It works. Ice Breakers are often fascinating speeches.

Subsequent speeches in the Toastmaster's basic manual emphasize different skillsets in speaking—organization, gestures, vocal variety, and the like. Often in doing these speeches, Toastmasters choose subjects of which they know little; they research a topic and give a speech laden with facts. The end result is a wooden, unenthusiastic presentation.

Over the years I have noticed that, often, Toastmasters get to their seventh or eighth manual speech before they again give a speech as good as their Ice Breaker. Why? Because they finally get back to choosing topics they care about and that they have personal experience with.

Specifically, they get back to

1. **Loving their subject:** only speaking about topics they really care about;

2. **Being themselves:** you can only be a second best somebody else;

3. **Telling personal stories:** making a point and telling a story. If people remember the story, they remember the point.

Then it hit me. My first big "Aha!" moment in Toastmasters. **Since the best speeches are Ice Breakers, we should strive to make *every* speech an Ice Breaker.**

"Aha!" Moment #2. Toastmasters is a means to reflect on life's events and draw meaning and lessons from them.

After my "Aha!" Moment #1, I started to make every speech I did an Ice Breaker. That is, every time I wrote a speech, I looked for how I could illustrate it with personal stories from my own life.

I have been speaking in public for a long time now. And for most of that time, my speeches have had a strong personal component.

Typically, I pick an issue that is dominating my attention. Something that is really bugging me.

Like the time I bought an aluminum shingle roof. I paid three times the price of an asphalt roof.

Why? Well …

1. because I believed the salesman's claim that this was the next thing in wonder roofs! And

2. because I believed, to paraphrase Polonius, that "costly thy roof as thy purse can buy … rich not gaudy."

The problem? The roof didn't work. Two years after it was installed, it started to leak. I didn't want to admit defeat. For five years I tried negotiating with the contractor who sold me the roof.

When that didn't work, I had another contractor replace the offending parts of the roof. It leaked worse than ever. I spent the next five years trying to get the second contractor to fix his job. That didn't work either!

Finally, I admitted defeat. We ripped the whole thing off, including 75 per cent of the plywood underneath, and put on an asphalt roof.

That episode, in all of its horror, is saved in my files. In making a speech out of it, I revisited everything that had happened. I organized it in my mind. When did I do what I did and why? What happened next? Who did what to whom and how?

Lessons learned?

1. Know your contractor.

2. Never be on the bleeding edge of technology.

3. Cut your losses. Don't throw good money after bad.

I save all my speeches. Originally, they were all in hard copy. Now I have them stored on my computer. Years of speeches reflecting on life's challenges, big and small, have left me a type of diary that chronicles events but also draws wisdom from them to guide me in my future actions.

And that led me to my **"Aha!" Moment #2**
Toastmasters is a means to reflect on life's events and draw meaning and lessons from them.

Which brings us to my "Aha!" Moment #3.
Toastmasters can help you to form deep and valuable friendships, friendships that you can fall back on when life throws you its inevitable curves.

For years now, whenever I speak, I have used the occasion to reflect on the challenges that life has thrown my way. I have shared my hopes and my fears, my successes, my failures, my strengths, my weaknesses, my knowledge, and my ignorance.

At the Toastmasters clubs that I have spoken at—and, most notably, at Bay Street Breakfast, where I have attended most of its 1,001 meetings—others have done the same thing.

So what happens when you meet weekly for an hour plus with a group of people with whom you regularly share confidences?

Well, you do improve as a speaker!

But, more importantly, and this is my

Aha! Moment #3:
Toastmasters can help you to form deep and valuable friendships, friendships that you can fall back on when life throws you its inevitable curves.

I think women have always known that! But I am a man, and I am a slow learner!

Conclusion

So let me recap my three biggest "Aha!" moments in Toastmasters:

1. **Since the best speeches are Ice Breakers, we should strive to make every speech an Ice Breaker.**

2. **Toastmasters is a means to reflect on life's events and to draw meaning and lessons from them.**

3. **Toastmasters can help you to form deep and valuable friendships, friendships that you can fall back on when life throws you its inevitable curves.**

All of which has led me to a fourth "Aha!" moment. Because I know that Bay Street Breakfast, my Toastmasters Club, has become a sanctuary for me … a harbour into which I can sail my sometimes-leaky ship when it has been battered by the hurricane rigours of life.

Not the only sanctuary (I do have other family and friends!), but an important one.

Here's to the next 1,000 meetings!

Madam Toastmaster!

CHAPTER 24

The 2011 Tōhoku earthquake and tsunami occurred at 14:46 JST on March 11, 2011. The magnitude 9.0–9.1 undersea megathrust earthquake had an epicentre in the Pacific Ocean, seventy-two kilometres east of the Oshika Peninsula of the Tōhoku region, and lasted approximately six minutes, causing a tsunami.

This was a speech I made to the Bay Street Breakfast Club about that earthquake.

LESSONS FROM JAPAN—2011

What Happened

On Friday, March 11, 2011, at 2:46 p.m. local time, a massive earthquake, 9.0 on the Richter scale, hit Japan. The epicentre was approximately 250 kilometres northeast of Tokyo, seventy-two kilometres off the east coast.

Seismologists estimate this was the most powerful known earthquake to hit Japan, and one of the five most powerful earthquakes in the world overall, since modern record-keeping began in 1900. The earthquake moved Honshu 2.4 metres east and shifted the Earth on its axis by almost ten centimetres.

The earthquake triggered extremely destructive tsunami waves of up to ten metres that struck Japan minutes after the quake, in some cases travelling up to ten kilometres inland.

More than fifty aftershocks followed, seven at least 6.3 on the Richter scale, the size of the quake that struck New Zealand on February 22. These are still ongoing.

The Human Impact

Authorities confirmed 9,000 deaths, 3,000 injured, and 13,000 people missing across the area, as well as over 125,000 buildings damaged or destroyed. At least three nuclear reactors suffered explosions due to hydrogen gas that had built up within their outer containment buildings.

Over 4 million households are without electricity, 1.5 million are without water, and 500,000 people are homeless.

It is the toughest and the most difficult crisis for Japan since the Second World War.

What normally happens in the aftermath of catastrophes?

For example, Hurricane Katrina, the Haiti earthquake, the Congo civil war?

- Rioting.

- Looting.

- Price gouging.

- Rape, murder.

Sociologists attribute these reactions to the alienation of large sections of society in the areas affected by the catastrophes.

Aftermath in Japan?

None of the above because "that's not the way Japanese people are." The Japanese have a sense of being first and foremost responsible to the community. Thousands of years of Japanese culture have bred a society that respects, and seeks to demonstrate the virtues of, courage, benevolence, politeness, honour, loyalty, and self-control.

Can we be more like them?

Absolutely!

How?

1. First, as Norman Vincent Peale said, "The more you lose yourself in something bigger than yourself, the more energy you will have." Stop worrying about yourself so much and worry about others more.

2. Second. Long before a disaster occurs, we need to build a society that minimizes social alienation. We need to think about and look after each other. If we look after others when they are in need, they will look after us when we are.

3. Third. When faced with a crisis, focus!

Our best emergency response professionals respond to crises by staying calm, assessing the situation, and taking the action with the best probability of success. Don't second guess why you are where you are. Deal with the situation that is presented. There will be lots of time for second guessing if and when you survive the immediate crisis.

Sully Sullenberger, the pilot who successfully landed US Airways Flight 1549 on New York's Hudson River back in January 2009, saving the lives of all 155 people on board, has his own thoughts on this. He said he:

1. Forced calm on himself.

2. Imposed order on what could have been chaos.

3. Load-shed. He ignored everything that wasn't the highest priority.

Conclusion?

Ladies and gentlemen. I hate to break it to you, but **we are all going to die!**

The question is, "Why do we live?" What greater good is served by your existence? As Friedrich Nietzsche said, "He who has a *why* to live can bear almost any *how*."

What is wrong with the world? What are you going to do about it? Now, focus and just do it!

Mr. Toastmaster!

CHAPTER 25

The George Keenan Award is given every year to an active Toastmaster who continues to serve and promote Toastmasters within the District and externally. The selection committee consists of past recipients who continue to be active District 60 Toastmasters. They select a candidate from all eligible nominations who also embody our Toastmasters values.

In 2011, I was honoured with the award. Definitely, a high-water mark in my time in Toastmasters and, indeed, in my life.

Receiving the George Keenan award from District 60 of Toastmasters International in 2011. That is Ross Mackay on my left.

THE GOOD OLD DAYS—
TAKE 2—APRIL 11, 2011

(on the occasion of receiving the George Keenan Award)

Thank you, District 60, from the bottom of my heart! This award means the world to me. And it has caused me to reflect on what Toastmasters means to me.

I originally joined a French language club in Quebec in 1969 because I wanted to improve my French, but I left later that year to go back to school in Ontario.

In 1972, I rejoined Toastmasters for three main reasons:

1. To keep my brain alive without having to take night school courses with their attendant exams,

2. To keep in touch with my brother, Stan, who was a member of Scarborough, and

3. I was single in the big city and it was something to do.

But whatever our other reasons might be, I think we all share one: we want to become better public speakers.

I stayed:

1. To keep my brain alive.

2. Because of the positive reinforcement. I gradually became a better speaker. I started feeling better about myself, more confident that I could handle situations, be they speaking situations or leadership situations, and

3. Many of my best friends were Toastmasters.

And I went to district conferences. One of the fixtures there was George Keenan, acting as parliamentarian and credentials chairman, always with a big smile and a warm greeting for all. At that time, he was probably the most recognized, and most beloved, Toastmaster in District 60.

He was my hero.

That was Toastmasters for me in the '70s. A stimulating, growth-enhancing, family.

Those were the good old days!

But I had a problem. Single when I joined Scarborough in 1972, by 1979, I was married with four children. Family obligations took precedence. I quit Toastmasters.

The good old days of Scarborough and Toastmasters were gone.

For the next eight years, I concentrated on my family and my career. But I missed the friendships, the mental stimulation, and the confidence building of Toastmasters. And my speaking abilities were becoming rusty.

So in 1987, I came back.

I still could not reconcile my schedule to Scarborough's, but I did find another club, Toronto Downtown, that met at a time and place that better suited me.

I well recall the first district conference I attended after returning to Toastmasters. George Keenan was looking after credentials. Even though I had been away from Toastmasters for eight years, he remembered me by name and even asked about my brother Stan!

George has always been a role model for me in what a good Toastmaster should be like. He was such a kind soul. I don't think he had any personal ambition. He was consummately interested in everybody else

Buddhists have the concept of a bodhisattva, a person who could achieve nirvana for himself but who stays behind to help others achieve it. That was George. Everybody's bodhisattva. If I could ever be half the Toastmaster and person that he was, I would be happy. George taught me to think of Toastmasters in a completely different way. I don't know if you ever knew him, Pat, but you would have liked each other, because George, like you, was in Toastmasters to serve.

And because of George, I am still in Toastmasters … to serve.

Toastmasters is bigger than all of us. By helping us communicate better, it makes the world a better place.

The good old days that I had in Scarborough are now a distant memory.

But the good times I am having at Bay Street Breakfast, at Toastmasters Clubs around the district, and at Toastmasters conferences like this one this weekend, are very much alive.

Thank you, District 60, for the incredible honour you do me in giving me this award. I shall treasure it always.

Congratulations to you all

- for joining Toastmasters and
- for all you do for this remarkable, world-changing organization.

But in all you do, do take the time to pause, reflect, and enjoy every minute you are together,

because,

trust me,

these are the good old days!

Mr. Toastmaster!

CHAPTER 26

A reflection I gave at a service at St. Mark's United Church in the summer of 2011.

ARE YOU A GOOD NEIGHBOUR?

The scripture read to us today by Nanci MacKenzie is known as the parable of the Good Samaritan. Jesus is described as telling the parable in response to a question regarding the identity of the "neighbour" God calls us to love.

It is one of my favourite passages from the Bible.

In the parable, a Jewish traveller is beaten, robbed, and left half dead along the road from Jerusalem to Jericho. First a priest and then a Levite, fellow Jews, come by, but both avoid the man by passing by on the other side of the road. Finally, a Samaritan, a person from another country despised by the Jews, comes by and helps the injured man, proving to be more of a neighbour to him than people from his own background.

Today I want to examine this parable and what it has to teach us about the difficulty of being a good neighbour.

Let me give you some historical context.

First, the road from Jerusalem to Jericho

In the time of Jesus, the road from Jerusalem to Jericho was notorious for its danger and difficulty, and it was known as the "Way of Blood" because of the blood that was often shed there by robbers.

Second, Jewish Culture

In Jewish culture in the first century of the Common Era, contact with a dead body was understood to defile a person. Priests were particularly enjoined to avoid uncleanness. The priest and Levite may therefore have assumed that the fallen traveller was dead and avoided him to keep themselves ritually clean.

Third, Samaritans

The Samaritans are, and were in Jesus's time, an ethnic and religious group related to the Jews. Samaritans claim their worship is the true religion of the ancient Israelites prior to the Babylonian Exile, preserved by those who remained in the Land of Israel, as opposed to Judaism, which they assert is a related but altered and amended religion brought back by the exiled returnees.

Samaritans were hated by Jesus's target audience, the Jews, who considered them to be half-breeds. The Samaritans felt the same way about the Jews.

Portraying a Samaritan in a positive light would have come as a shock to Jesus's audience. It is typical of his provocative speech in which conventional expectations are turned upside down.

Today, the story is often recast in a more modern setting where the people are in equivalent social groups known to interact uncomfortably. In this way, the parable regains its message to modern listeners: namely, that an individual of a social group they disapprove of can exhibit moral behaviour that is superior to individuals of the groups they approve of.

For example, imagine a young Canadian lying hurt on Yonge Street, moaning. And imagine that a Canadian Liberal and a Canadian New

Democrat walk by on the other side of the street and ignore him but an American Republican, a right-wing supporter of George Bush and Sarah Palin, no less, is the one to stop and help him. Wouldn't that make you stop and think?

How Do You Justify Leaving a Man to Die on the Side of the Road?

On April 3, 1968, Martin Luther King Jr., in his "I've Been to the Mountaintop" speech, said:

"And you know, it's possible that the priest and the Levite looked over that man on the ground and wondered if the robbers were still around. Or it's possible that they felt that the man on the ground was merely faking, and he was acting like he had been robbed and hurt in order to seize them over there, lure them there for quick and easy seizure.

And so, the first question that the priest asked, the first question that the Levite asked, was, 'If I stop to help this man, what will happen to me?' But then the Good Samaritan came by, and he reversed the question: 'If I do not stop to help this man, what will happen to him?'"

King was in Memphis that day to support the sanitation workers who had been on strike. He was aware he was risking his life. But he said the question is not, "If I stop to help this man in need, what will happen to me?"

"If I do not stop to help the sanitation workers, what will happen to them? That's the question."

The next day, he was shot to death.

That's the bad news. Being a Good Samaritan can be risky. It can even cost you your life.

The good news is that the strike ended on April 12, 1968, with a settlement that included union recognition and wage increases.

In his best-selling book, *The Tipping Point*, Malcolm Gladwell recounts a study at the Princeton Theological Seminary. Researchers asked each seminarian "to prepare a short, extemporaneous talk on a given biblical theme, then walk over to a nearby building to present it. Along the way to the presentation, each student ran into a man slumped in an alley, head down, eyes closed, coughing and groaning. The question was, "Who would stop and help?"

The researchers included three variables:

1. the background of the subject— whether they had entered seminary as a way of helping people or not,

2. which parable they were to prepare—several were given the Good Samaritan parable as their subject, and

3. a time context, saying either that they were running several minutes late and should hurry up, or that they were early and had some time to spare.

The results were astonishing. The first two variables had no effect. Whether somebody had devoted their life in service to their fellow man or had just been reminded of the value of altruism by preparing a speech on the Good Samaritan had no effect on if they stopped and helped. "The only thing that really mattered was whether the student was in a rush. Of the group that was in a hurry, 10 per cent stopped to help. Of the group who knew they had a few minutes to spare, 63 per cent stopped."

So what does that study at Princeton tell me?

It tells me that I should not be too quick to dump on the priest and the Levite for being such rotten people. They were probably no better or worse than the rest of us.

So What Do I Do?

I met my wife, Julia, in 1972. On our first real date, I took her to the Toronto production of *Godspell*, a musical based on the life of Jesus that was playing at the Royal Alex.

I wore my pink and blue suit, but that's another story!

As we were about to enter the theatre, we were aware of a beggar accosting people outside the theatre. I was torn. Should I give him money or not? What would my date think of me if I did? What would she think of me if I didn't? I passed by on the other side feeling cheap and embarrassed.

Fifteen minutes later, we were sitting comfortably in our seats and the show started. Jesus came out on the stage. Guess who was the actor playing Jesus? Right the first time! The beggar from the front of the theatre!

Ever since then, the image of that beggar at the front of the theatre has been burned into my consciousness.

For thirty-four years I went to work at King and Bay Streets. On a typical day, as I walked between Union Station and Scotia Plaza, I would see two or three people begging for money.

That upset me, especially in winter, when the people in question have obviously slept the night over the grates on the north-east corner of Bay and Wellington or in front of the Design Centre in the old stock exchange building.

That, I thought, could be me there. What can I do to help them? If I put a toonie in their Tim Hortons coffee cup, would it help? And if I didn't, what kind of a human being am I? And always I thought of that beggar at the front of the theatre.

I usually still don't give the beggars any money. I do support our church and the Mission and Service Fund and the United Way and Habitat for Humanity.

But I still wonder,

Am I not more like the priest and the Levite than the Good Samaritan?

And what about you? Are you a good neighbour?

Amen.

CHAPTER 27

In July 2011, our son Ross married Evi Siregar in Medan, Indonesia. She is a wonderful lady and we were delighted for both of them that they found each other. My wife, Julia, had to remain in Canada because she does not respond well to long plane trips and because our first granddaughter was arriving in July and she wanted to be there to help our son Doug and his wife, Jessica, with the new baby. I went with my brother Stan, his wife, Mary, and our two nephews, Mike and Gord.

Shortly after I got back, I was scheduled to do a service at our church, one of the summer congregational replacements when our minister was on vacation.

Scripture:

Matthew 18:15–20 English Standard Version (ESV)

[15] "If your brother sins against you, go and tell him his fault, between you and him alone. If he listens to you, you have gained your brother.

[16]But if he does not listen, take one or two others along with you, that every charge may be established by the evidence of two or three witnesses. [17]If he refuses to listen to them, tell it to the church. And if he refuses to listen even to the church, let him be to you as a Gentile and a tax collector.

[18]Truly, I say to you, whatever you bind on earth shall be bound in heaven, and whatever you loose on earth shall be loosed in heaven. [19]Again I say to you, if two of you agree on earth about anything they ask, it will be done for them by my Father in heaven.

[20]For where two or three are gathered in my name, there am I among them."

Micah 6:8 English Standard Version (ESV)

[8]"He has told you, O man, what is good; and what does the LORD require of you but to do justice, and to love kindness, and to walk humbly with your God?"

CONVERSATION: WHAT DOES THE LORD REQUIRE OF YOU?

What does the Lord require of you?

As many of you know, our son Ross married Evi, a lovely Muslim girl, in Indonesia last July. I was there for the wedding.

I had several chats with Evi's mum and dad over the course of my three-week stay in Indonesia. They are good Muslims, but I am convinced that their views on God are not that different from mine, and not that different from Micah's admonition: "What does the Lord require of you but to do justice, and to love kindness and to walk humbly with your God?"

About a week after I got back, a Christian friend and neighbour forwarded an email to me that said, among other things:

"I'm tired of being told that Islam is a 'religion of peace' when every day I can read dozens of stories of Muslim men killing their sisters, wives, and daughters for their family 'honour,' of Muslims rioting over some slight offense; of Muslims murdering Christians and Jews because they aren't 'believers,' of Muslims burning schools for girls, etc., etc., etc., all in the name of Allah, because the Qur'an and Sharia law tells them to."

It was not the first such email I have received from this friend, who regularly sends me many emails. The great majority of his emails are fascinating and/or humorous.

Unfortunately, the Islamophobic sentiment of some of them seems all too common in the post 9/11 universe. Some people blame Islam and all Muslims for the horrific acts of a few terrorists. One such person was the Norwegian Anders Behring Breivik who, on July 22, 2011, massacred seventy-seven innocent Norwegians in Oslo to show his hatred of Muslims. Talk about a disconnect!

After the Breivik massacres, Haroon Siddiqui, the *Toronto Star* columnist, wrote that:

"… we are witnessing a furious attempt by Islamophobic politicians and pundits, as well as their apologists, to decouple themselves from Anders Behring Breivik, the Norwegian terrorist … They, of course, do not advocate violence, while he is a mass murderer. The distinction is clear enough. But they influenced him and shaped his worldview."

We need to be careful with the words we use.

Could I have a volunteer from the congregation please?

Now, I have some toothpaste here and a bowl. Please squeeze the toothpaste out of the tube and into this bowl.

OK. Is it all out? Now, I need someone else to put the toothpaste back in the tube. Any volunteers?

No takers? Why not?

Because it is far more difficult to put toothpaste back in the tube than it is to squeeze it out.

Our words are like that. They can come out of us so easily, but they cannot be put back.

So words should be chosen wisely.

Carelessness in our choice of words can hurt people deeply. Sometimes, it can unwittingly encourage people to do terrible things.

I thought about today's scripture reading from Matthew before speaking to my friend.

Jesus said, "If your brother sins against you, go and tell him his fault, between you and him alone. If he listens to you, you have gained your brother." I also remembered there have been all too many times when *I* have engaged my own mouth before my brain was in gear!

I reminded my friend that I now have Muslims in my family. I told him that I was tired of blanket condemnations of Muslims or any other religious, ethnic, linguistic, or cultural group. I told him that God knows some Muslims have done bad things but so have some Christians, Sikhs, Hindus, and Buddhists, etc. We had a good chat. He assured me that he did not subscribe to the views of the email and apologized for forwarding it to me. I have not received any similar emails from him since.

What does God require of us? Micah said that God has told us what is good.

All that God requires of us is to do justice, and to love kindness, and to walk humbly with our God.

May God help us to do just that!

Amen

CHAPTER 28

My brother Bruce died peacefully in a Peterborough, Ontario hospital from MS on September 15, 2011, after a lengthy illness. He was sixty-three. The funeral and interment service for Bruce, together with the interment service for my dad (Dad had died two years earlier), were held in Oakville, Ontario on a rainy morning on September 29, 2011. Our son Doug, a United Church minister, performed the service. I did the eulogy. I call it:

UNCLE BRUCE

 My brother Bruce was a free spirit who enjoyed life to the full while he was healthy. Much of that life he shared with his partner, Carole. About twenty-five years ago, Bruce was diagnosed with multiple sclerosis, a degenerative disease of the nervous system for which there is no known cure. Sadly, the MS caused the relationship with Carole to founder; they split fifteen years ago. And, of course, it was the cause of his untimely death.

As many of you know, my son Ross is in Indonesia and was unable to get home for this service. He sent me this note.

Hi, Dad,

I'm not sure how or where you'd use this,
or even if you should,
but given that I won't be there for the service,
I'd at least like to share with you who Bruce was to me.

And I'll start it with a joke:

On Remembrance Day
many years ago,
a small public school invited a World War II veteran
to talk to the children about his memories of the war.
With the auditorium filling up with children,
the teacher received word
that their guest had to cancel at the last minute
and she paced frantically,
trying to figure out what she was going to do.

Seeing their elderly Polish janitor
sweeping the floors down the hallway,
she ran up to him and asked him
if he was in the war

and if he'd mind
speaking to the children about some of his
experiences.

He confirmed he had served with the air force
and would be happy to speak.

He stepped into the auditorium
and up to the microphone.
"In 1942," he said slowly,
"the situation was tough.
The Germans had a very strong air force.

I remember ..." he paused.

"I remember one day we were flying,
protecting the bombers,
and suddenly,
out of the clouds,
five Fokkers appeared below us!
So we dived down and I aimed at one of the Fokkers
and fired a burst from my machine guns
right into him
and he exploded.

Then I saw that one of the Fokkers was on my tail,
so I pulled round in a loop
and got behind him,
fired,
and he went down in a fireball.

I looked around
and saw two Fokkers attacking my squadron leader,
so I slipped in behind them, fired,
and that was another Fokker in flames.

The next Fokker tried to get away from me,
but I got right up behind him,

blasted him with my machine guns,
and he turned over and exploded!

There was only one more Fokker left,
and he was now trying to get away!
But I flew up behind him, SHOT—
BABABABABABABA. BOOOOooooooommmmm …"

The teacher,
who'd been listening and watching in horror,
interrupted at this point.
"Children, I should point out
that 'Fokker' was the name of an airplane
used by the Germans in the war."

"That's true," said the janitor,
"but these Fokkers were flying Messerschmitts!"

I think I was twelve, maybe fourteen,
when Bruce told me this joke,
and it was the first time an adult had shared
something with me that was so unfiltered.

You and Mom had sent me and Jenn
to Carole and Bruce's cottage in Tweed for a
weekend in the summer,
and he told us this
while the four of us sat on their porch,
and it was great.

My entire time there was incredible.
We swam in the river,
went canoeing,
watched old movies,
and the two of them never spoke down to us
but rather with us.
They shared as friends and not as aunt and uncle.

Growing up, I felt distant a lot of times,
awkward and unsure of myself,
but around Bruce and Carole, this all disappeared.

They laughed at my jokes,
listened to my stories,
didn't treat me like an annoyance, and,
in a time in my life
when I sometimes felt that I didn't belong,
I had a place around them.

I think it was in 1995,
before I went to Trent,
you told me that Bruce had gotten into a car
accident
and the doctors found that it was due to MS,
but I dismissed it out of ignorance.

I didn't know what MS was.
Bruce wasn't hurt in the accident.
No need to worry.

Not long after,
two weeks into my first year at Trent,
I called Grandma and Grandpa to say hello,
and they invited me over for dinner
with them and Bruce.
Bruce was there?
Wonderful!
I hadn't seen him in a while,
and I was so eager for a chance to catch up.

Grandpa and Bruce welcomed me at the college
and I jumped in the back seat of the car.
Bruce was sporting a brand new thick,
scruffy beard.

I made a passing comment
on how I liked his new lumberjack look,
but it wasn't until we arrived back at the house,
and I saw that Bruce needed help
getting out of the car and inside,
that I truly realized the gravity of his situation.

I think I made it about halfway through dinner before
excusing myself.
I disappeared around the corner
and cried like a child.

Over the past few years,
we've all watched him deteriorate,
and you and Grandma have been kind in saying
that I connected with him during this time,
but I see it differently.

When I visited Bruce in the hospital
and looked into his eyes,
in some ways I saw myself,
and I owed him an unfiltered conversation
as he'd shared with me so many times before.

I think to some extent
Bruce was one of my first, best friends.

Incidentally,
Bruce and Carole's neighbour in Tweed had a dog
that frequently marked his territory all over their
property.
Carole told us that the week before Jenn and I
arrived,
Bruce had walked around their cottage
and pissed on all the trees to reclaim it.

On a side note,
in the chance that Carole does attend the funeral,
please give her a hug from me.

Love, Ross.

I told Ross that his grandma said to me recently
that one of the things she loved about my dad,
Ross's grandpa,
was that any time his kids asked him a question,
he would give the grown-up answer;
he never talked down to us.

Ross's brother-in-law, Bagus,
said in his comment to me about Bruce's passing:
"He has not passed away, Rob.
He lives in the hearts he leaves behind."

Ross's story shows better than I could ever say
the truth that Dad lived on in Bruce,
and they both will live on in our hearts
for as long as we live.

Amen.

CHAPTER 29

A reflection I gave at our church, St. Mark's United, in November 2011.

WHY ST. MARK'S IS IMPORTANT TO ME

1 Amazing grace, how sweet the sound
that saved a wretch like me!
I once was lost, but now am found,
was blind, but now I see.

2 'Twas grace first taught my heart to fear
and grace my fears relieved;
how precious did that grace appear
the hour I first believed!

What speaks to me about these verses?

As a child, I found they set an impossibly high bar over which I could never hope to jump.

We moved a lot when I was a boy. Wherever we lived, we joined a nearby church and attended services there on Sunday. I went to Sunday School and I learned the Bible stories, including the parables of the Prodigal Son and the Good Samaritan.

Some churches we attended came from the John 3:16 school of theology: "For God so loved the world, that he gave his only begotten Son, that whosoever believeth in him should not perish, but have everlasting life."

Typically, these churches spelled out what they meant by "believing in him" in the Apostles' Creed, or variations on it. That is,

> "I believe in God the Father Almighty,
> Maker of heaven and earth:
> And in Jesus Christ his only Son our Lord,
> Who was conceived by the Holy Ghost,
> Born of the Virgin Mary; etc., etc., etc."

Now, if that works for you, God bless you! But I took no comfort from John 3:16 because:

1. I found the Apostles' Creed unbelievable, and

2. I could not understand why God, the same God of the Prodigal Son and the Good Samaritan, would only forgive our sins if we believed this—to me—incredible story.

As a boy, I always had questions. No answers … just questions.

- What is God?

- What are we here for?

- Who cares?

- Is this all there is?

- What do I believe?

As an adult, I trained as an engineer and worked for thirty-four years as a banker. I am a skeptic of the first order; I like things I can touch and hold on to. But I find reality just as hard to believe as any miraculous story in the Bible:

- Unseen signals in the ether are mysteriously converted into sounds from our radios and cell phones and pictures on our TVs, BlackBerries, and iPhones.

- $E = MC^2$

- The universe, with billions of stars in each of billions of galaxies, started some 15 billion years ago from nothing.

So I had problems with my beliefs as a child. But, as they say, "It gets better!"

As I grew in age and, I hope, wisdom, my beliefs changed to incorporate views from many different sources, including people at St. Mark's and at other churches I have attended, authors of books I have read over the years, friends and relatives of every faith community you can imagine, and my own reflections on all of the above.

I am now sixty-five and I have answered all of my youthful questions to my own satisfaction—maybe not to yours! But to mine!

With these answers, grace has appeared, and my fears have been relieved because I now believe! ☺ I once was lost, but now am found, was blind, but now I see!

What is God?

I believe, as Neale Donald Walsch said, God is our highest, best thought.

What are we here for?

I believe we are here to love each other wastefully without counting the cost. In this we can follow the excellent example of Jesus of Nazareth.

Who cares?

I care. I believe St. Mark's cares. I believe God cares.

Is that all there is?

Yes, I believe that is all there is. The rest is commentary.

I see signs of vibrant life everywhere I look in St. Mark's. I would not want to mention any particular area lest I inadvertently leave someone or something out; I feel St. Mark's has, for many years, striven to love others wastefully without counting the cost.

That is why I came here.

That is why I am content here, and

That is why I hope to stay here, happily engaged, for many years to come.

Amen

CHAPTER 30

A reflection I delivered in September 2012.

PASTORAL CARE TRUMPS THEOLOGY

A Story of Our Faith James 1: 17–27 (New Revised Standard Version) (read by Julia Peck)

"Every generous act of giving, with every perfect gift, is from above, coming down from the Father of lights, with whom there is no variation or shadow due to change.

In fulfilment of his own purpose, he gave us birth by the word of truth, so that we would become a kind of first fruits of his creatures.

Hearing and Doing the Word

You must understand this, my beloved:
let everyone be quick to listen, slow to speak, slow to anger;
for your anger does not produce God's righteousness.

Therefore, rid yourselves of all sordidness and rank growth of wickedness, and welcome with meekness the implanted word that has the power to save your souls.

But be doers of the word, and not merely hearers who deceive themselves.

For if any are hearers of the word and not doers,
they are like those who look at themselves in a mirror;
for they look at themselves and, on going away, immediately forget what
they were like.

But those who look into the perfect law, the law of liberty, and persevere, being
not hearers who forget but doers who act—they will be blessed in their doing.

If any think they are religious, and do not bridle their tongues but deceive
their hearts, their religion is worthless.

Religion that is pure and undefiled before God, the Father, is this: to care
for orphans and widows in their distress, and to keep oneself unstained by
the world."

PASTORAL CARE TRUMPS THEOLOGY

Thank you, Jane, for that magnificent solo of "Amazing Grace"!

2 'Twas grace first taught my heart to fear
and grace my fears relieved;
how precious did that grace appear
the hour I first believed!

This hymn talks about the importance of "believing."
"To believe" in something is defined as
"to have confidence or faith in the truth of" that something.

So to what did John Newton,
the author of "Amazing Grace,"
refer when he said "the hour I first believed"?

Presumably, he was referring to the Apostles' Creed:

> "I believe in God,
> the Father almighty,
> Creator of heaven and earth,

and in Jesus Christ,
his only Son, our Lord,

who was conceived by the Holy Spirit,
born of the Virgin Mary,

suffered under Pontius Pilate,
was crucified, died, and was buried;

he descended into hell;
on the third day he rose again from the dead;
he ascended into heaven, etc., etc."

And, as soon as he believed that, Newton knew he was going to heaven!

4 The Lord has promised good to me,
this word my hope secures;
God will my shield and portion be
as long as life endures.

Full disclosure: I don't know about you,
but every so often I think about the fact
that one day I will eventually die,
and I am scared.

So I am very interested in buying into any way
that would make my death less scary.
Getting into heaven would solve my problem!
But while I have always loved the hymn "Amazing Grace,"
the music touches my very soul,
despite years of trying,
I couldn't bring myself to believe that Jesus
was the "only Son, our Lord, conceived by the Holy Spirit etc., etc."

So what worked for Newton did not work for me.
Which is why I like James so much!

James says that, at some point, all the talk stops and actions follow.
Religious actions ought to have the same concerns

as religious language—care, justice, fairness, protection of the vulnerable, respect, and, of course, love.

James said, "Show me your faith without your works,
and I will show you my faith by my works." [1]

Undoubtedly
the most influential debate in the course of Christian history
is "faith vs. works."
It was the cause of the Reformation,
as Luther's opinion on the matter
differed from the Roman Catholic Church.

The argument has been around for almost two thousand years.
The argument,
very basically,
is about how people are saved from their sins
so they can go to heaven when they die.

Both Paul and James wrote about it,
Paul arguing for the saving power of faith,
James arguing for the saving power of good works.

So which is better: "faith" or" works"?

I like to think the faith vs. works debate is meaningless,
a complete red herring!
Because the two words mean the same thing:
that we should try to live more like Jesus lived.

I like to think that when Jesus called people to have faith in him and to believe in him, he meant he wanted them to give their hearts to what he considered important—specifically, loving your neighbour.

That thought is reflected in a poem, "Abou Ben Adhem," by the great English poet Leigh Hunt, published in 1834, which has been a favourite of mine since I was first introduced to it in Grade 10:

Abou Ben Adhem (may his tribe increase!)
Awoke one night from a deep dream of peace,

And saw,
within the moonlight in his room,
Making it rich, and like a lily in bloom,

An angel writing in a book of gold: —

Exceeding peace had made Ben Adhem bold,
And to the Presence in the room, he said,
"What writest thou?"
—The vision raised its head,
And with a look made of all sweet accord,
answered "The names of those who love the Lord."

"And is mine one?" said Abou.
"Nay, not so," replied the angel.
Abou spoke more low,
But cheerly still,
And said
"I pray thee, then,
Write me as one that loves his fellow men."

The angel wrote, and vanished.

The next night It came again with a great wakening light,

And showed the names whom love of God had blessed,

And lo!
Ben Adhem's name led all the rest.

Or as Kathryn Moase's dad, Cliff Moase, is fond of saying, "Pastoral care trumps theology!

Amen!

CHAPTER 31

HAPPY WIFE, HAPPY LIFE

We bought our house thirty years ago, in 1983. Perfect house, I thought. Good location. Great neighbours. Four plus one bedrooms. Nice lot.

I loved the house. Everything about it.

Julia too. Except for the kitchen!

Almost from the day we moved in, Julia would complain about it.

Problems with the Old Kitchen

1. Layout

   - The fridge door bumped into the peninsula

   - Minimal counter space—and Julia loves to cook. There was no room to roll out pastry, no room to chop up vegetables.

2. Cupboard hinges

   - Stuck out half an inch at forty-five degrees to the corners of the cupboards. So when you leaned over to roll out your pastry, fifty-fifty you gashed your head on a hinge!

3. Everything was past its best before date

   - Cupboards were made of plastic and cracking. They were patched together with duct tape!

   - The linoleum on the floor was cracking. But then the rug covered up most of that ... most of the time!

   - The laminate countertops were chipped, cracked, and burnt. But at least they were flat!

   - In March of 2012, the stove died. The oven element had gone for the second time. And the front of the stove got so hot when the oven was on that people got second-degree burns from bumping into it. That was enough of a problem if Julia was the one being burnt. But down the road with grandchildren coming along, that could get really serious.

   - The faucets at the kitchen sink were shot.

   - Water leaked from around the sink into the cupboard below.

   - The wallpaper was old, marked, and peeling

Relevant Facts

<u>Fact #1:</u> For twenty-nine years, my wife complained about that kitchen.

<u>Fact #2:</u> Our previous house had an incomplete kitchen that was only finished the week before we listed the house. We never got to enjoy it.

<u>Fact #3:</u> In 2012, we received an inheritance that meant we could afford to fix the kitchen.

<u>Fact #4:</u> We could not realistically sell the house in the condition it was in.

<u>Fact #5:</u> If we were going to fix up the kitchen, this time we wanted to do it long enough before we sold the house so we could enjoy it too!

So we hired a contractor and, six months later, we got this!

Here's the new kitchen, living room, and dining room.

Now you might notice that the project grew beyond the kitchen. That was my fault!

First, we knocked the wall out between the kitchen and the living room.

That meant we had to redo the living and dining room and hall floors … and ceilings!

And that meant we had to redo the front steps …

... and railings!

We've now been living in our dream kitchen for six months.

We blew every penny of our inheritance on it, and we don't regret it! We keep pinching ourselves and saying, "This is ours!"

And in all those six months, I haven't heard Julia complain about her kitchen once!

Happy wife, happy life!

Mr. Toastmaster!

CHAPTER 32

A speech to my Toastmasters club in 2014.

IN PRAISE OF KEEPING AT IT

"Your work is to discover your world and then, with all your heart, give yourself to it."
—Buddha (563 BCE–483 BCE)

There is value in spending your life sampling a bit of this and a bit of that. Also, a cost.

I tried the former as a child and youth. I moved more than ten times before I was twenty, living in five different countries.

I was born in Toronto sixty-eight years ago.

When I was a year old, we moved to Guyana … actually, it was called British Guiana then.

When I was three, we moved to Switzerland.

When I was four, we moved to England.

When I was eight, we moved to Quebec.

When I was eleven, we moved to Oakville.

When I was seventeen, I moved to Switzerland.

When I was eighteen, I moved to Denmark.

Then I went to school in Kingston, Ontario, where I moved every September and every summer until graduation.

All of these moves are broadening, yes, but limiting too, because just when you have scratched the surface, you move on.

Since my twenties, I have tried the other side. In my residence, job, and other interests, I have chosen to plant my flag and stay. This has the advantage of allowing me the time and means to learn the good, and the not-so-good, points of my chosen place. That done, I can reinforce the good points and mitigate the others.

Case in point: for the last thirty-one years, I have lived at 43 D'Arcy Magee Crescent in Scarborough.

Now don't get me wrong … I have always loved our house. Great neighbours. Great location close to work, close to family, close to major highways. The house itself is structurally sound. Nice yard.

But we have had issues!

For example … the kitchen.

For the first twenty-nine years at 43 D'Arcy Magee, we lived with a 1960s-era kitchen. You know what I mean—chipped linoleum tile floors; burnt and cracked Arborite countertops; copper tone, non-functioning range hood; chipped and broken cabinets; and old, mismatched appliances.

So in 2012, we took action. We gutted the kitchen, knocked out walls, redid the floors and ceilings, and bought all new appliances (including a functioning range hood!).

We love the result!

Second example: the deck.

We had a nice cedar deck that my son Ross and I built sixteen years ago, but it was definitely past its best before date. The upper level was a bit too narrow to fit a dining table comfortably, and the cedar decking was starting to rot. The choice was between Plan A—redoing the whole thing in composite—and Plan B—replacing five or six boards every year. We went for Plan A! Ross, my son-in-law, Murrey, and I did the framing, and TMF Contracting did the decking, railing, and lighting.

Here's the Before

Here's the During

And here's the After

Again, we are thrilled with the result!

That's the house.

But as I see it, the same lessons apply to the rest of our lives. Whenever a relationship, a job, or other situation (**and, yes, that does include Toastmasters!**) does not perfectly suit our desires, we are faced with the temptation to cut our losses and move. The problem with that approach, as I see it, is two-fold:

1. even if we know what we want, we don't know what we need, and

2. there is no realistic chance that what we want and need will be sitting on a platter waiting for us to take it.

The alternative, of course, is to identify those areas that fall short and move to correct them.

Since my twenties, I have chosen the latter course. As I see it, the end result is that I live in a world that suits me admirably because I had a hand in creating it! **And, yes, that does include Toastmasters!** As Robert Schuller has said, "If it is going to be, it is up to we. And if it is up to we, it is up to me!"

So if you are a dabbler who enjoys tasting a little of everything life has to offer, go for it! Yes, and do report your findings back to the rest of us so that we can share vicariously in your education.

But when you have mapped your universe, revisit the high points of your tour and delve into them more deeply. Or, as Buddha said, "Discover your world and then, with all your heart, give yourself to it."

Mr. Toastmaster

CHAPTER 33

Colleen C. Smith
1992–2015

Julia's cousin, Colleen Claire Smith, twenty-two, of Riverview, New Brunswick, passed away at the Moncton Hospital on Sunday, May 24, 2015. At her request, I did the eulogy.

COLLEEN SMITH

We shouldn't be here. It is just not fair. For someone to die at just twenty-two years of age is horrible. It breaks our hearts. There's no good reason this happened. Colleen did nothing to deserve the pain she lived with her whole life. Kim and Ellen did nothing to deserve the heartbreak of losing their beloved daughter. We are all so sorry.

That said, her life was a blessing. To her family, to her friends, and to the world at large. Into a life that was far too short, Colleen packed ten lifetimes of suffering. But she also packed ten lifetimes of courage and wisdom and warmth and love.

That is a tribute to Colleen. It is also a tribute to her amazing parents, Kim and Ellen. Parents who loved and nursed her through the years. Parents who recognized and celebrated her special gifts. Parents who let her be who she wanted to be and do what she wanted to do.

Kim and Ellen, you raised a spectacular daughter. Without you, Colleen would not have become the incredible woman she was. Without you, I have no doubt we would all be much poorer in spirit than we are today.

For you gave us Colleen.

So what was she like?

1. **Colleen treasured her friends and held them close.**

   Larissa was Colleen's classmate from kindergarten through Grade 6 and a lifelong friend. Larissa is lactose-intolerant. Any time Colleen was preparing food for Larissa, she would make sure that nothing containing milk products was anywhere in Larissa's sight.

   When exchanging presents, what she received was not as important to Colleen as the joy on her friends' faces when opening their presents.

   Larissa remembers that no matter how sick she was, Colleen was always smiling. From this, Larissa learned that no matter what life throws at you, there are usually ways to get through it. If you can't change it, you might as well be happy.

   And Colleen taught her friend Alyson that we should not take life for granted. We must really cherish friendship because sometimes that is all we have.

2. **Colleen loved life.**

If Colleen did anything, she did it with gusto. Her cousin Krista and Uncle Rick remember how competitive she was in playing "BLURT" or any other game.

Cathy Beardsworth, Colleen's teacher in Grade 6, worried about her going out to the bus on her own. She had to negotiate stairs and there were lots of big, rambunctious boys in the school that Cathy feared might inadvertently knock her over. Cathy said she needn't have worried. Colleen had good elbows and would never let anyone knock her over!

And she was never timid in class. If she didn't know something, she would ask. She was tremendously respected by the other students, a fact attested to by the number of her former classmates who are with us here today.

Cathy's husband, Paul, taught Colleen in Grade 12 and was struck both by her devotion to her course work and by her willingness to berate other students if they distracted her and other serious students from their work.

Cathy and Paul agree that anyone who taught Colleen for a year came away from the experience in awe of her spirit. You could not help but respect her zest for life.

3. **Colleen was brilliant.**

If you haven't yet read Colleen's poem that is on display at the front, I urge you to do so after we break later for pop and pizza. It is hard to believe those wise and profound words came from a girl who was only sixteen years old at the time.

Her friend Carrie remembers that when they were younger, Carrie would go with Kim, Ellen, and Colleen to visit Colleen's Grandpa Austin and Grandma Clare at their farm in Salisbury. On the car ride there, Colleen used to listen to her Walkman and sing along with the music, all the time reading her latest book. And not miss a beat!

She was a voracious reader. Everyone knows her favourite store was Chapters. Her apartment at home was awash with the fruits of her many visits to that holy shrine. Indeed, many people have observed that if Chapters declares bankruptcy in the near future, it will be because of the steep drop in their business due to Colleen's passing.

4. **Honest.**

Alyson says Colleen was the most honest person she has met in her entire life. One day, Alyson changed her profile picture on Facebook. The next day, Alyson went to visit Colleen at the hospital. Colleen said, "I loved the picture, but the lipstick's gotta go!"

Another time, Alyson went with Colleen to see the movie, *The Fault in Our Stars*. Everyone who knows the movie knows you are going to be crying because it is about two teenage lovers who both have cancer.

Who here has not seen the movie? Spoiler alert! The boyfriend ends up dying!

And relevant fact: every time Colleen and Alyson would see a sad movie, Alyson always cried and Colleen would say, "I don't know why you are crying. It is not really that sad!"

So they go to the movie and, you guessed it, Alyson was sobbing at the end. Colleen's reaction? Total embarrassment that her friend was crying so hard. She insisted that Alyson accompany her to the washroom so that no one could see that her friend was crying.

Sometimes that honesty hurt, but Alyson always knew that Colleen meant well; everything Colleen said, she said with love and with heart.

5. **Colleen was tough as nails.**

When Colleen was six, her babysitter, Becky, took her to the park to the swings and gave her an "under-ducky." Who here knows what an "under-ducky" is? I didn't know, either! That's when you push someone on the swing, running under them so that they go up really high.

You guessed it! Colleen wasn't ready and she fell. She never cried.

But here is her honesty again; she never let Becky forget what she had done! And afterward, whenever they went to the park, she always told Becky, "No under-duckies!"

I don't know if Becky ever told Kim and Ellen about that accident!

Colleen inspired all who knew her: her friends, her family, her teachers, her caregivers. They all compared the hurdles Colleen had to overcome in her life with those they had to face. They all ended up thinking, *Certainly no one else that I have known in my life has faced anything close to the challenges she faced head on. If she can do this, then I can too!*

6. **Colleen was focused.**

Carrie recalls how Colleen was set in her ways; she knew what she wanted, and she went after it.

Stacey recalls that Colleen wanted you to be punctual; if you said you would pick her up at a certain time to take her to Chapters, then you jolly well should be there at that time.

One day, Becky was cooking on the stove with Colleen and had to turn to tend something nearby. She told Colleen not to touch the stove because it was hot. What did Colleen do? Right the first time! She touched the stove and burnt her hand! But she didn't blame Becky! She admitted she had to find out for herself what a hot stove felt like!

In summary.

In her short life, Colleen learned how to live life with great distinction.

She taught us all

1. To treasure our friends and hold them close.

2. To love life.

3. To be honest in your dealings with others.

4. To focus on what is important to you.

Those things are all within our control.

Some other things, not so much. We cannot all be as brilliant as Colleen. We cannot all be as courageous as her. But we have all been given gifts by our creator to a greater or lesser degree. If we are to properly honour Colleen's memory, we need to develop those gifts as best we can and to share them with the world.

Do it for Colleen.

CHAPTER 34

I gave this speech in 2015.

Eric Arthur Blair (25 June 1903–21 January 1950), who used the pen name George Orwell, was an English novelist, essayist, journalist, and critic. He is best known for his 1945 allegory, *Animal Farm*, and his 1949 dystopian novel, *Nineteen Eighty-Four*.

Orwell's work continues to influence popular culture, and the term Orwellian, referring to totalitarian practices, has entered the language, together with several of his invented words, such as Cold War, Big Brother, doublethink, and thought crime.

This is an abridged version of Orwell's essay, "Why I Write."

Two interesting side notes:

1. Orwell wrote this essay in 1946, the year I was born, after he wrote *Animal Farm* and before he wrote *Nineteen Eighty-Four*.

2. Orwell died on my birthday four years later.

Coincidence?

WHY I WRITE

From a very early age, perhaps the age of five or six, I knew that when I grew up, I should be a writer.

Between the ages of about seventeen and twenty-four, I tried to abandon this idea, but I did so with the consciousness that I was outraging my true nature and that, sooner or later, I should have to settle down and write books.

I was the middle child of three, but there was a gap of five years on either side, and I barely saw my father before I was eight. For this and other reasons, I was somewhat lonely, and I soon developed disagreeable mannerisms which made me unpopular throughout my schooldays. I had the lonely child's habit of making up stories and holding conversations with imaginary persons, and I think from the very start my literary ambitions were mixed up with the feeling of being isolated and undervalued.

When I was about sixteen, I suddenly discovered the joy of mere words, i.e., the sounds and associations of words. As for the need to describe things, I knew all about it already. So it is clear what kind of books I wanted to write, in so far as I could be said to want to write books at that time.

I wanted to write enormous naturalistic novels with unhappy endings, full of detailed descriptions and arresting similes, and also full of purple passages in which words were used partly for the sake of their own sound.

I give all this background information because I do not think one can assess a writer's motives without knowing something of his early development. His subject matter will be determined by the age he lives in — at least this is true in tumultuous, revolutionary ages like our own—but before he ever begins to write, he will have acquired an emotional attitude from which he will never completely escape.

Putting aside the need to earn a living, I think there are four great motives for writing, at any rate for writing prose. They exist in different degrees in every writer, and in any one writer the proportions will vary from time to time, according to the atmosphere in which he is living.

They are:

   1. *Sheer egoism.*

Desire to seem clever, to be talked about, to be remembered after death, to get your own back on the grown-ups who snubbed you in childhood, etc., etc.

2. *Aesthetic enthusiasm.*

Perception of beauty in the external world, or, on the other hand, in words and their right arrangement.

Pleasure in the impact of one sound on another, in the firmness of good prose or the rhythm of a good story.

Desire to share an experience which one feels is valuable and ought not to be missed.

3. *Historical impulse.*

Desire to see things as they are, to find out true facts and store them up for the use of posterity.

4. *Political purpose.*

Using the word "political" in the widest possible sense.

Desire to push the world in a certain direction, to alter other peoples' idea of the kind of society that they should strive after.

It can be seen how these various impulses must war against one another, and how they must fluctuate from person to person and from time to time.

I am a person in whom the first three motives would outweigh the fourth.

In a peaceful age, I might have written ornate or merely descriptive books, and I might have remained almost unaware of my political loyalties. As it is, I have been forced into becoming a sort of pamphleteer. First, I spent five years in an unsuitable profession (the Indian Imperial Police, in Burma), and then I underwent poverty and the sense of failure. Then came Hitler, the Spanish Civil War, etc. By the end of 1935, I had still failed to reach a firm decision. The Spanish war and other events in 1936–37 turned the scale, and thereafter I knew where I stood.

Every line of serious work that I have written since 1936 has been written, directly or indirectly, *against* totalitarianism and *for* democratic socialism, as I understand it. It seems to me nonsense, in a period like our own, to think that one can avoid writing of such subjects. It is simply a question of which side one takes and what approach one follows. And the more one is conscious of one's political bias, the more chance one has of acting politically without sacrificing one's aesthetic and intellectual integrity.

What I have most wanted to do throughout the past ten years is to make political writing into an art.

My starting point is always a feeling of partisanship, a sense of injustice.

When I sit down to write a book, I do not say to myself, "I am going to produce a work of art." But I could not do the work of writing a book, or even a long magazine article, if it were not also an aesthetic experience.

Anyone who cares to examine my work will see that even when it is downright propaganda, it contains much that a full-time politician would consider irrelevant.

The job is to reconcile my ingrained likes and dislikes with the essentially public, non-individual activities that this age forces on all of us.

In one form or another, this problem comes up again. The problem of language is subtler and would take too long to discuss. I will only say that of late years I have tried to write less picturesquely and more exactly. In any case, I find that by the time you have perfected any style of writing, you have always outgrown it.

Animal Farm was the first book in which I tried, with full consciousness of what I was doing, to fuse political purpose and artistic purpose into one whole. I have not written a novel for seven years, but I hope to write another fairly soon. It is bound to be a failure, every book is a failure, but I do know with some clarity what kind of book I want to write.

Looking back through the last page or two, I see that I have made it appear as though my motives in writing were wholly public-spirited. I don't want to leave that as the final impression. All writers are vain, selfish, and lazy, and at the very bottom of their motives there lies a mystery.

Writing a book is a horrible, exhausting struggle, like a long bout of some painful illness. One would never undertake such a thing if one were not driven on by some demon whom one can neither resist nor understand. And yet it is also true that one can write nothing readable unless one constantly struggles to efface one's own personality.

Good prose is like a windowpane. I cannot say with certainty which of my motives are the strongest, but I know which of them deserve to be followed. And looking back through my work, I see that it is invariably where I lacked a political purpose that I wrote lifeless books and was betrayed into purple passages, sentences without meaning, decorative adjectives and humbug generally.

THE END

Three years after writing this essay in 1949, George Orwell published his classic novel, *Nineteen Eighty-Four*.

He died in 1950.

Mr. Toastmaster

CHAPTER 35

In 2015, I was sixty-nine. It is an age when increasingly we are aware that many of the people who were with us when we arrived in this world are leaving us to carry on without them. That prompted this speech to my Toastmasters club.

HOW TO WRITE A EULOGY

The Oxford dictionary defines a eulogy as "A speech or piece of writing that praises someone or something highly, especially a tribute to someone who has just died."

You are a Toastmaster. That means that sometime, maybe sooner, hopefully later, a family member or friend is going to ask you to do a eulogy for someone who has died. Someone who was dear to you both.

This is a great honour and a great responsibility. It is also a great opportunity. It is a chance for you to:

- relieve the anxiety of the person who asks you,

- honour the person who has passed, and

- help the grieving family and friends come to terms with their loss.

Because my family and friends know I am a Toastmaster, I have been asked to do more than my share of eulogies. Most recently for Colleen, the daughter of my wife's cousin. Indeed, I have been asked to do so many eulogies that I have developed a twelve-step methodology for writing them! Today I am going to share that methodology with you in the hope that it can help you out in a stressful time.

So here goes:

1. Get all the information you can about the deceased in the days or weeks before the funeral service.

2. Don't organize it. Just put it down in point-form notes. You will be changing it later!

3. If the service is out of town, it is best to stay in a hotel rather than with family or friends. That way, you have more freedom to work on your eulogy and less temptation to socialize. First things first.

4. Make sure the hotel you are staying at has a business centre or other facility for typing and printing word documents. If you have a laptop, even better; you can work in the comfort of your hotel room.

5. Ideally, the visitation is on the day before the service proper. Get there early and stay late! The visitation is the best place to talk to people because many people will be present who would not other-wise be available to talk to.

6. Talk to as many people who knew the deceased as you can. At the visitation for Colleen, I had extra assistance. Her aunt and uncle told many of her family and friends that I was looking for information about Colleen to do my eulogy; they asked them to think about anecdotes that would describe Colleen and to share them with me. That was a **huge** help.

7. Take a steno pad with you. Take extensive notes. Ask everybody:

   - How did you know the deceased? For example, were they a relative, friend or co-worker?

   - What was your most vivid memory? Why? When? Where? How?

8. If yours is the only eulogy, you are speaking for all present. Submerge your own persona. Certainly, your relationship to the deceased is important—it is, after all, why you are doing the eulogy—but the content of the eulogy should be about the deceased and the memories the other attendees at the service have about him or her. The more your eulogy reflects their common experience, the better they will feel.

9. Stay up as late as required to assemble these notes into some, indeed any, logical order. Look for common themes and group them together. Be honest but be gentle. If in doubt, leave it out!

10. Be prepared to throw anything out if it doesn`t seem to fit. In the eulogy for Colleen, I ended up throwing all my early notes out. The stuff I used all came from my conversations with people at the visitation the night before the service.

11. Look at it again in the morning and tweak it.

And finally,

12. If the death was premature, feel free to say, "This is wrong. We shouldn't be here." That was very helpful advice I received from the minister at my church. Funeral services for older people are often legitimately seen as celebrations of long lives well lived; after all, everyone will die eventually. But it seems unfair when people die young.

Nevertheless, at whatever age a person dies, their lives have meaning and purpose. It is our job as eulogists to make sure their loved ones know the life that is now ended was not in vain.

Colleen was born with a medical condition that almost guaranteed she would die young. Indeed, it was a triumph of sorts that she managed to live as long as she did.

I started my eulogy for Colleen as follows:

We shouldn't be here. It is not fair. For someone to die at just twenty-two years of age is horrible. It breaks our hearts. There's no good reason this happened. Colleen did nothing to deserve the pain she lived with her whole life. Kim and Ellen did nothing to deserve the heartbreak of losing their beloved daughter. We are all so sorry.

That said, her life was a blessing. To her family, to her friends and to the world at large. Into a life that was far too short, Colleen packed ten lifetimes of suffering. But she also packed ten lifetimes of courage and wisdom and warmth and love.

After Colleen's service, one of her friends asked her aunt about me and was told I was a Toastmaster. She said every family should have one! I can think of no better compliment for a Toastmaster! So if you have ever wondered why you joined Toastmasters, now you know one reason!

As Maya Angelou said, "People will forget what you said. People will forget what you did. But people will never forget how you made them feel." Eulogies are important. Done well, they help people get through one of the most difficult times in their lives. Your family and friends will thank you, and you will always be proud that you were there for them in their time of need. So if you are asked to do a eulogy, do it for the person who asked, do it for the person who has passed, and do it for the family and friends of the deceased. But, most especially, do it for yourself!

Mr. Toastmaster

CHAPTER 36

A reflection I did at our church in August 2016.

THE GOODNESS OF HUMANITY

It has been a pretty gruesome past couple of months. Massacres. Police killings of innocent people. Reprisal killings of innocent police. Politicians blaming entire races and/or religious groups for some or all of the above. It is enough to make one lose their belief in the goodness of humanity.

Seventy-five years ago, Viktor Frankl was a prisoner at both Auschwitz and Dachau. It's fair to say he had as good a reason as any to have lost his belief in the goodness of humanity. Yet he wrote these words of his experience:

"Our generation is realistic, for we have come to know man as he really is. After all, man is that being who invented the gas chambers of Auschwitz; however, he is also the being who entered those gas chambers upright, with the Lord's Prayer or the Sh'ma Yisrael on his lips."

Pause for brief commercial message: St. Mark's Book Study group will be studying Frankl's book, Man's Search for Meaning, from January to May next year. Stay tuned for further information in the fall. We now return to our regularly scheduled programming!

As gruesome as the news can appear today, it is good to remember that news media, by their very nature, concentrate on the shocking and horrific.

It is **not** considered news that, around the world today, millions of people got up, made their breakfast, kissed their kids and sent them off to school, and kissed their spouses and went off to work.

It is **not** considered news that, elsewhere in the world, people planted gardens, went for bike rides, went on vacations, got married, had children, helped their neighbours, stopped at traffic lights, and generally obeyed the law and were nice to others.

One of my guilty pleasures is reading obituaries of people who have lived good lives. On July 24 I read the obituary of Ursula Franklin.

Ursula was born in Germany in 1921 and came to Canada in 1949 as a post-doctoral fellow at the University of Toronto with a PhD in experimental physics. She was a scientist, a feminist, a Quaker, a pacifist, an activist, and a treasured mentor to many.

Ursula's family said that Ursula was a proponent of the "earthworm theory"; that is, it is the little acts that prepare the soil and nurture the seedlings so that bigger actions can follow and flourish. They asked that, in Ursula's honour, people consider small acts that will make the world and our society a better place.

Today, I want to reflect on how we can each offset the terrible news we see in our various media with our own random acts of kindness.

Indeed, we can make a difference; we have the power to restore people's belief in the goodness of humanity ... not by extraordinary deeds of bravery and/or generosity, but by relatively small, random acts of kindness.

Some examples:

1. **Everyone is important.**

   Catherine, do you remember the last time someone called you by name?

   The clerk at the chiropractor's office always calls me by my first name. It always makes me feel good.

I now make a habit of calling people by their first names. It is often easy to do because at the bank, at Starbucks, and at many other locations, clerks wear name badges with their first names on them. Learn the names of your office security guard, the person at the front desk, and other people you see every day. Greet them by name. Say "hello" to strangers and smile. These acts of kindness are easy, and they almost always make people smile.

2. **Give someone the benefit of the doubt.**

   If you're upset, take a deep breath and count to twenty, slowly, before you say anything. Ask yourself if what you're going to say will be helpful. Pausing will reduce the likelihood you'll say something you will regret. Remind yourself that a positive mindset is a choice **you** can make.

   Last year I was parking my car and saw a perfectly able-bodied man of forty-something park in a handicapped parking spot. It upset me. I told him I thought it was wrong for him to park in the spot … that it was reserved for people with disabilities.

   He smiled gently and said, "I know. I am picking up my handi-capped mother!"

   Oops! Lesson learned!

3. **Follow up.**

   Cancer victims often report receiving tremendous support when first diagnosed with the disease but find the support tapers down while they go through their lengthy treatments. Hearing this makes me feel guilty because I know I haven't been thoughtful enough myself about long-term follow-up. But now I'll try to do better.

   Let's remember to reach out and comfort people months after a trauma like disease, divorce, or death.

As Maya Angelou said, "I've learned that people will forget what you said, people will forget what you did, but people will never forget how you made them feel."

How do you define success?

Dictionary.com defines it as a noun meaning:

1. the favourable or prosperous termination of attempts or endeavours; the accomplishment of one's goals;

2. the attainment of wealth, position, honors, or the like;

3. a performance or achievement that is marked by success, as by the attainment of honours: *The play was an instant success*;

4. a person or thing that has had success, as measured by attainment of goals, wealth, etc.

During the 2010 Zheng-Kai marathon in Zhengshou, China, Jacqueline Nyetipei Kiplimo of Kenya saw a Chinese elite disabled athlete struggling to drink water. She ran with him from the 10km to the 38km mark, aiding him through all the water stations. She sacrificed winning and $10,000 to be a true hero. This simple act of humanity cost Jacqueline a first-place finish.

She was not successful in being first this time. But as David W. Orr, a noted environmentalist, has said:

"The plain fact is that the planet does not need more 'successful' people. But it does desperately need more peacemakers, healers, restorers, story-tellers, and lovers of every kind. It needs people who live well in their places. It needs people of moral courage willing to join the fight to make the world habitable and humane. And these qualities have little to do with success as we have defined it."

The **butterfly effect** is a term used in chaos theory to describe how small changes to a seemingly unrelated thing or condition (also known as an initial condition) can affect large, complex systems.

The term comes from the suggestion that the flapping of a butterfly's wings in South America could affect the weather in Texas, meaning that the tiniest influence on one part of a system can have a huge effect on another part.

This is good and bad. Someone does a little mean thing and it can have immeasurably harmful consequences. But imagine what happens if someone does something nice; somebody feels better and does something nice for several other people.

They each feel better and do something nice for several others. It snowballs and, before you know it, the world is an immeasurably nicer place!

What it comes down to is, we can all make a difference. An incredible difference! We can collectively be the reason that people believe in the goodness of humanity!

So let's go make a difference!

Do it for Ursula Franklin!

Do it for Jacqueline Kiplimo!

Do it for humanity!

Amen!

CHAPTER 37

THE GOOD OLD DAYS – TAKE 3 – 2017

I often remember the good old days when my dad and I would talk about stuff. It might have been about school. About problems with friends. About stuff.

Dad died nine years ago in 2009 of colon cancer just short of his ninety-first birthday. He had a long life. Many challenges, but if you make it to ninety-one, it is hard to complain.

That said, the last few years were difficult. He had a number of strokes, some minor, one major. And the colon cancer was demeaning and restrictive.

In addition, Mum and Dad lived in Peterborough, an hour's drive from our home in Scarborough, which made visits inconvenient.

The net result was I did not have many satisfying chats with Dad in the last years of his life. Looking back, I regret that profoundly. I always felt close to Dad. Perhaps closer to him than to my mum since, after all, we were both male and there was some physical resemblance. I studied engineering at school because Dad was an engineer and I wanted to be like him. That proved to be a bridge too far … we were not **that** much alike, and I was not cut out for engineering … but I did end up taking an MBA, and we had many chats over the years about management techniques and philosophies.

A year after Dad died, Mum went into a retirement home in Peterborough. Her church and many friends were there, and it was good for her not to have to worry about maintaining the house and to have the extra help with meals and housekeeping.

Mum had four sons. My brother Bruce died of MS in 2011. My youngest brother, Weston, lives three hours north of Peterborough. My older brother, Stan, and I live in Toronto. As Mum got older, it became more difficult for her to get herself around, and my brothers and I had to travel to Peterborough to take her to doctors' appointments. This meant limited time to visit with Mum, as we needed over two hours to commute to Peterborough and back, plus the time for the doctor's visit plus the time to commute to the doctor's office. For Weston, there was an additional four hours of commuting required. For all practical purposes, a visit to Mum required each of us and our spouses to allocate an entire day.

Mum is now ninety-seven. She has few friends left in Peterborough, and she is suffering from some dementia.

Dementia is an overall term for a set of symptoms that are caused by disorders affecting the brain. Symptoms may include memory loss and difficulties with thinking, problem-solving, or language, severe enough to reduce a person's ability to perform everyday activities.

Mum has significant memory loss, and her logic is sometimes faulty. She does not always remember to take the pills she needs to take and is often confused as to the names and relationships of family members. She is not as aware of personal hygiene requirements as she should be.

A year ago, her GP in Peterborough told us it was time for Mum to go into long-term care. That is, a nursing home.

If your family member is accepted for long-term care in Ontario, you are allowed to pick up to five nursing homes that you would find acceptable. Then you put your name on a list and wait. We were told that the wait time for Mum would be five to eight months from the date of our application. When an opening in one of those homes becomes available, you have twenty-four hours to accept or reject the offer. If you accept the offer, you have up to five days to move in. If you refuse the offer, your application to **all** chosen homes will be cancelled. In such a case, you cannot re-apply for twelve weeks after the day you were removed from the waiting list, unless there is a significant change in your condition or circumstances.

On September 29, 2017, nine months after our application, we were advised that Mum had been accepted by Bendale and we had until Monday, October 1, 2017, to accept or reject the offer.

We accepted.

On Tuesday, October 2, 2017, we moved Mum into Bendale. It took another two weeks to move all her stuff out of her retirement residence. Some went to Bendale, some went to family members, some went to charity, some went into storage in our house, and some went to the dump.

What a wonderful decision it has proven to be! In long-term care

1. Doctors come to the residents. Residents don't have to go to the doctors. So when we visit Mum, none of our time is used up taking her to see her doctors.

2. Nursing and personal care is provided twenty-four-seven. Some people think that keeping people in their own home is preferable to having them in a nursing home. I respect those views. But do you want to change your mum's diapers? Do you want to bathe her? Are you available twenty-four-seven?

3. Personal hygiene/medical/clinical/bed linens/laundry supplies are provided.

So we no longer have to allocate an entire day to visit Mum. Where in recent years I had been seeing Mum once, sometimes twice, a month, I now see her five or six times a week. And in less total time. Now in a typical day, I drive fifteen minutes to Bendale, visit Mum for thirty minutes to an hour, and then drive fifteen minutes back home—total elapsed time: less than two hours!

Make no mistake, Mum still has dementia. She still has some memory loss and difficulties with logical thinking, problem-solving, or language. But I am convinced that with all of that she still has lots of memory that works just fine and there is lots of logic in much of what she thinks and talks about. We do have long, meaningful chats. Moreover, I am convinced that:

- our visits are keeping her mind more active than it otherwise would be, and,

- we are delaying the advance of her dementia.

Now I have time to get into all kinds of subjects with Mum. We reminisce about past family events, we talk about my kids and our challenges, we talk about my life, about Toastmasters, church, you name it. In short, all the things I have always wished I had discussed with Dad during his last years.

For Mum and me, these are the good old days!

Mr. Toastmaster.

Mum in 2017

Mum and Dad in 2007.

CHAPTER 38

This was a reflection I gave at Bay Street Breakfast Toastmasters Club after Ian Miller, a beloved member of our club for many years, died in 2018.

IN PRAISE OF IAN SCOTT MILLER

MILLER, Ian Scott, CA, CPA, passed away surrounded by family at home on September 25, 2018. A memorial service took place at Harcourt United Church in Guelph, on Saturday, October 13.

Ian is survived by his wife of fifty-four years, Edna, his children, Heather, Kyle, and Drew and their families, and a host of friends around the world, including many members of the Bay Street Breakfast Club.

Ian was raised in Montreal and subsequently moved, first to Ottawa, then to Toronto.

I first met Ian some forty years ago when we worked on the same floor at Scotiabank, but I didn't get to know him well until 1990, when we were both founding members of the Bay Street Breakfast Toastmasters Club, which the bank sponsored.

For the next twenty-three years, Ian and I were in almost daily contact. Each week we would meet at Toastmasters. After our meeting we would often chat for a while about family, politics, and the United Church of Canada, of which we were both proud members.

Before Ian and I retired from the bank, we would often meet for lunch in the bank cafeteria. These chats with Ian were an important part of my life, a sanctuary from the often-stressful life of a banker.

After retirement, Ian continued to use his accounting skills as auditor for the Eagle Lake Property Owners Association (ELPOA) for his favourite retreat at the family cottage and as treasurer for the Village by the Arboretum Residents' Association (VBARA) in Guelph.

Church was important to Ian, and he was active in congregations wherever he lived.

What I loved about Ian is what everyone loved about Ian.

1. He was a really good person. How so?

   • He was warm and kind.

   • He was gentle and loving

   • He maintained friendships and supported many people with his positive attitude and his zest for life. He was empathetic, always thinking of others. For example, when our youngest son needed someone to sign his passport application, Ian was there. When our second son needed help processing his application for non-resident status, Ian was there. Ian was always there when we needed him.

2. He was endearing.

   • He loved all things Scottish; he could recite Robbie Burns' "Address to the Haggis" by heart.

   • He loved puns. They were incessant, often real groaners, but you had to love them!

   • What made him especially endearing to me was that he loved the same kind of humour that I did! Like the British musical comedians, Flanders and Swan (Think the hippopotamus song:
   "Mud, mud, glorious mud!

Nothing quite like it for cooling the blood.
So, follow me, follow
Down to the hollow,
And there let us wallow
In glo-o-o-orious mud!")

And the British comedy troop, Beyond the Fringe! Think I always wanted to be a judge:

"Yes, I could have been a judge
But I didn't have the Latin.
I never had sufficient Latin for the judging exams.

"They are very rigorous, the judging exams. They are noted for their rigour. People come staggering out of the judging exams shouting, 'O, my God, what a rigorous exam!'

"So, I became a coal miner instead.

"They're not very rigorous, the mining exams. There is a complete lack of rigour.
In the mining exams.
They only ask you one question; they say, 'Who are you?' and I got 75 percent on that!"

3. With all of that, Ian had a deep side. He was

- Keen to learn.

- Eager to engage in deep and serious discussions and debates.

- Witty and energetic (he could deliver a witty speech, to the point, with humour and the occasional pun or two, with introspection and without ego).

Five years ago, our connection was loosened when Edna and Ian moved to Guelph, but we still kept in touch.

A good person. An endearing person. A deep person. I miss him.

God bless you and keep you, Ian, until we meet again.

CHAPTER 39

PECK, Margery Upton Margery lived a fulfilling life, sixty-five years with her beloved husband, Bob, deceased 2009. After a short time in palliative care, she passed away on Sunday, March 24, 2019, six weeks shy of her ninety-ninth birthday. She was the proud mother of Stan (Mary), Rob (Julia), Bruce (deceased), Weston (Cathy), and the late infant Janet. Grandma to Michael (Stacey), Gordon (Alaina), David (Fay), Ross (Evi), Jennifer (Murrey), Douglas (Jessica), Graham and Linda (Lee). She is survived by eleven great-grandchildren. In 1973, Bob and Margery retired to Peterborough, attending Trent University to earn honours degrees, hers in modern languages. Always gracious, she cared for her mother, Clara Upton, her son Bruce, and her husband, Bob. She treated her sons' wives as if they were daughters and was much loved by them. The family thanks the staff of Applewood Retirement Residence in Peterborough and Bendale Acres Long-Term Care Home in Scarborough for their excellent and loving care. Friends are welcome to join us for a graveside Celebration of Life at Oakville/St. Mary's Pioneer Cemetery, 659 Lyons Lane, Oakville, at 11 a.m., on Wednesday, April 24, 2019. A reception will follow at St. John's United Church in Lusk Hall at 262 Randall Street, Oakville.

CLARA MARGERY UPTON PECK

The following is the eulogy I read at my mum's Celebration of Life at Oakville's St. Mary's Pioneer Cemetery on April 24, 2019.

Thank you all for coming today. It means a lot!

As my dad, Bob Peck, was my hero, my mum, Margery Peck, was my heroine, the "white hat" who performed great deeds and selfless acts for the common good.

How and why did Mum become such a heroine?

Nature and nurture.

Nature in that she was born healthy and smart.

And nurture:

- nurture by her grandparents, her parents, and her aunts and uncles;

- nurture by Dad and his parents; and

- nurture by the church communities that formed a critical part of her support network throughout her life.

The net result was that Mum loved life:

- She was kind:

She loved her family: She cared about us all. Her love, and Dad's, was always unconditional; they would often say, "Just remember, no matter what happens, we love you and we are proud of you!" Whenever we parted, she would say, "Now you take care! You are important!"

And she loved other people: people at church, people at the hospital where she volunteered, people at Dad's work, neighbours, people everywhere.

- She was a life-long learner:

She earned a university degree in home economics as a young woman in 1941. She taught herself French, Danish, and German when the family's travels took her to other countries. Then she earned a second and third university degree in modern languages in her sixties. She was a talented seamstress. For example, she sewed and smocked gorgeous dresses for her granddaughters.

- She was faithful:

She followed Dad down to Guiana during the war to marry him. And followed him everywhere thereafter, supporting him and the family as Dad's work and circumstances took us to Ontario, to Guiana again, to Switzerland, to England, to Quebec, to Ontario again (that would be Oakville!), to Denmark, to England again, and again back to Ontario.

And that was just the homes we lived in! She also followed him on business and vacation trips to many other places around the world.

And everywhere they moved, Mum and Dad joined a local church and were involved in the church and community.

- She was active:

Fencing at university, curling in her thirties. Travel in her teens, twenties, thirties, forties, fifties, sixties, seventies, and eighties. Tai Chi in her seventies and eighties.

Mum was pragmatic.

She was sensible, realistic, and practical. She was strong mentally, emotionally, and physically. The Depression and the Second World War taught her to deal with things as they were rather than as she wished them to be, and she motored through life full steam ahead, rarely complaining.

While she had medical challenges of her own, she never let that get in the way of looking after Dad, who had more medical challenges than a cat has lives. When our sister Janet died as an infant, when Dad died after years of courageously fighting cancer, when our brother Bruce died after a long, courageous fight with MS, she mourned, yes, but she got on with life, enjoying her remaining children and their families and her other friends.

When asked in her later years if she felt her treatment in life had been unfair, she said, "No."

"Why me?" she asked? She answered her own question: "Why not me?"

Maya Angelou, the American poet, storyteller, and activist, said, "I've learned that people will forget what you said, people will forget what you did, but people will never forget how you made them feel."

Maya also said, "Your legacy is what you do every day. Your legacy is every life you've touched, every person whose life was either moved or not. It's every person you've harmed or helped. That's your legacy."

Mum's legacy is in every one of her children and their families; her legacy is in the people she made feel good, throughout her life, in the many communities in which she lived and moved.

We are only here for a short time. Wherever you are, whoever you are with, love life, be kind, and make people feel good!

Do it for Mum! Do it for Margery! Do it for yourself! Because, as Mum would say, "You are important!"

It will be your legacy.

Amen.

CHAPTER 40

A reflection I did at our church in August 2019.

GRATITUDE

Let us pray:

Holy Spirit, may my words help people to discover what they seek and provide a link for them with the Sacred.

Amen.

These days, I find myself overwhelmed with feelings of gratitude. This morning I want to look at my gratitude for Canada, my family, my friends, nature, and my good health.

When I was born seventy-three years ago, Jews, people of colour, and women were not allowed on the boards of major corporations or as members of many organizations.

Today, they are. Today, as I walk around downtown Toronto, diversity is everywhere. Everyone is a minority: whether you are white, Black, brown, red, yellow, or pink, whether you are male, female, or in-between, whether you are old or young, straight or gay: there are thousands of people just like you passing you on the street. That makes me feel secure … I don't think that any group I encounter feels threatened or threatening.

Canada is a more inclusive society today than it has been at any time in its history.

I am grateful for Canada!

I come from a family with five children. Life has its tragedies. My sister Janet died as an infant when she was only a few months old, and my brother Bruce died at sixty-three of MS. Through it all, Mum and Dad raised us all with love and understanding, and the rest of us have survived to live productive lives.

Julia and I have, in turn, had four children, each of whom pulls their weight in society.

Families can be frustrating, annoying, and heartbreaking. They can also be loving, supportive, and heart-warming!

I am grateful for my family!

And friends. Hardly a day goes by that Julia and I don't do something with our friends from St. Mark's United Church. We both attend Sunday worship and Book Study and Bible Study groups. Julia is involved in the choir and the Knit and Natter Group. But we also socialize with our friends from St. Mark's in other venues.

Toastmasters. Most Wednesday mornings, find me with my friends at the Bay Street Breakfast Toastmasters Club. Many of us have known and supported each other for years ... even decades!

Neighbours. Julia and I have lived in the same house for thirty-six years and the same neighbourhood for forty-five years. Many of our neighbours have been here even longer. Those relationships have been honed over untold cups of coffee and borrowed sugar. We've borrowed snowblowers in the winter and garden umbrellas in the summer. We've attended each other's weddings and funerals.

Church, Toastmasters, neighbours, and classmates from school and colleagues from work: I am grateful for my friends!

Recently, I drove my son Ross and his family to Pearson airport for an early morning flight. As I was driving back home at 5:30 a.m., I saw the sun rising in the east, painting the clouds everchanging shades of pink, purple, and orange. It was wonderful to behold.

Once a week, I walk down to the GO train station at 5 a.m. to go to my early morning Toastmasters meeting. In the process, I am guaranteed to see at least four bunnies hopping across my path. Not to mention squirrels, robins, and raccoons.

Coming home, I will see blue jays, cedar waxwings, the occasional Baltimore oriole, and hawks.

We are surrounded by the beauty of nature.

I am grateful for nature!

I am seventy-three and, as far as I know, in good health. My two grandfathers died at the age of fifty-nine. Any walk through a cemetery gives me lots of evidence that many people in the past did not get the biblical three score years and ten. I have already beaten the odds.

I survived childhood! I did some pretty crazy things as a kid.

For example, when I was eight to ten years old, we lived next to a train track that ran two kilometres down the line past my school. Freight trains shunted down the tracks at slow speed. We would hop onto the freight cars and ride the trains to school!

And train trestles ... at the same age, my friends and I would walk five hundred metres on a one-track train trestle, two hundred metres above the valley floor. Thank God we never met a train while we were crossing!

And in my early twenties I went parachuting after only three hours of training.

Any one of those exploits could have seriously injured or killed me.

Some of my friends weren't so lucky. John dove into a shallow lake when he was twenty-two and has been a paraplegic for the last fifty- years. Why was I spared? I don't know.

Medicine has never been more advanced than it is today. Canada has a medical system that foots the bill for much of our health-care requirements. The help I really need has, so far, been readily available. That is not true for everyone, and the system can be improved, but relative to one hundred, or even fifty, years ago, we have come a long way.

I am grateful for my good health!

The net result?

1. I have places where I feel safe, comfortable, wanted, and, yes, needed.

2. I have lived longer than the historical average. From here on in, I am playing with house money!

For all of the above, I am grateful!

My situation is probably representative of many, if not most, people at St. Mark's.

Many of us have crosses to bear, but most of us have much to be grateful for.

So how do we express our gratitude?

Surely, it must be by paying it back.

How? Many of the people who have helped get us to where we are today are no longer around.

The solution must be to pay it forward.

And how do we do that? I'm a firm believer that the first thing we have to do is look after ourselves; you can't pour water from an empty cup.

When we are stressed out, self-care is often the first thing we let go of.

So first, do something nice for yourself.
Sit in the back of the church and just worship.
Read a book.
Go out for a nice meal.
See a movie.
Have a warm bath or shower.
Listen to nice music. Call a friend on the phone.
Join a support group.

Self-care is not self-indulgence; it is self-preservation.

Then when your cup has water in it, pour!

Do something for others. Donate your money. More importantly, donate your time. At St. Mark's. At your favourite charity. In your neighbourhood.

Show your gratitude!

Amen!

CHAPTER 41

I wrote this speech in 2021 for the Club International speech contest. I won the club contest but lost at the area, the next level of the Toastmasters annual contest, which culminates in the World Championship of Public Speaking.

YOU WILL RISE!

You may shoot me with your words,
You may cut me with your eyes,
You may kill me with your hatefulness,
But still, like air, I'll rise.

Those words were written by Maya Angelou. My purpose today is to share with you how she modelled what we all have to do to rise above our difficulties and have a good and meaningful life.

Maya was born in St. Louis, Missouri, in 1928. When she was eight, her mother's boyfriend raped her. She told her brother, who told the rest of her family. The courts convicted the rapist but only jailed him for one day. Four days after his release, he was murdered, probably by her uncles.

As a result, she became mute for five years, because, she said: "I thought, my voice killed him; I killed that man, because I told his name. And then I thought I would never speak again, because my voice would kill anyone."

During this period of silence, she developed an extraordinary memory, a love for literature, and a knack for observing the world around her.

By the time she died in 2014, she had become a poet, a writer, an actress, a director, and a producer, and was respected as a spokesperson for Blacks and for women.

I would add, speaking as a white man that I, and countless others, honour her, regardless of our colour or gender!

With her courage in rising above her problems as a Black woman in a racist, misogynistic society, with her awareness of others' suffering, and with her brilliant mind, she developed insights that have inspired people around the world to make their countries better places for themselves, for their children and for their children's children!

Today I want to share with you two examples of Maya's insights.

First,

Maya wrote:

I've learned that people will forget what you said,
people will forget what you did,
but people will never forget how you made them feel.

I have a personal example of the truth of that comment:

My mother died two years ago. On a Sunday—coincidentally, the first Sunday that Daniel, our new minister, preached at our church. There was cake to be served after the service to celebrate Daniel's first day with us. This was before COVID-19. The service started at 11 a.m. and lasted for an hour.

We were fifteen minutes into the service when Mum's long-term care home called to say my wife, Julia, and I, should get there right away. We were there in another fifteen minutes, but Mum had already died.

It was hard.

We did not expect to see anyone from church, but at 12:30 p.m., Daniel walked into the room! You could have knocked me down with a feather! He must have grabbed his cake, said a few words to the congregation, and come right over.

I don't remember what he said. I just remember that he listened to us and he cared.

He was newly married and had his wife, Merriam, at home, but he didn't look at his watch. He just chatted with us. I was so grateful.

After about forty-five minutes, I looked at my watch and said to him, "Daniel, Merriam must be wondering where you are." He smiled at me and said, "Merriam knows I am where I need to be!"

God, I love that man!

Second,

Maya's remarks on legacy.

Maya's good friend and protégée, Oprah Winfrey, tells the following story:

I'd just returned from the opening of my school in South Africa and was regaling Maya with all the details. "This school will be my greatest legacy," Oprah said. "It will impact generations to come."

Maya stopped her cold.

"You have no idea what your legacy will be!" she said. "Your legacy is every life you touch! It's every person who ever watched your show and felt something. Was moved to do something. Go back to school, leave an abusive marriage, stop hitting their kids.

"It's not one thing—it's everything!'"

Note that Maya was not speaking about Oprah's legacy for Black women! She was speaking about her legacy for all people! Directly and indirectly,

Maya touched millions, including Oprah, Nelson Mandela, Kamala Harris, the new vice-president of the United States, and, yes, me!

What should you take from all of this?

First:

People will forget what you said,
people will forget what you did,
but people will never forget how you made them feel.
And how you helped them to rise!

Second:

Your legacy is every life you have ever touched. And it is exponential, because it extends to everyone touched by everyone you have touched, and everyone touched by them!

And long after you have gone from this mortal plane, like Maya Angelou, still, you will rise!

Mr. Toastmaster!

EPILOGUE

In the last twenty-five years, I have learned that nobody is perfect; we are all a work in progress, in our character and in our speeches. There is real value for us in recording our thoughts on the issues important to us and revisiting them from time to time to see whether we have changed our minds, or should.

I have further learned:

On Speeches

- Speeches can be great if they are simple, sincere, contain personal stories about the speaker, are presented confidently, and are spiced with humour.

- We can reuse our good stories in many different ways, in many different speeches, to illustrate many different points.

- Anyone can give a great speech. We just need to do it, get feedback, and then do it again. And again. And again.

- People don't have to be in Toastmasters to become better speakers, but like chicken soup for a cold, it can't hurt.

- Preparing a speech on a subject is a wonderful way to work out how we really feel about it.

On Religion, Ethics, and Happiness

- Rudyard Kipling said you are a good person if you can keep your head when all about you are losing theirs and blaming it on you, and if you can trust yourself when others doubt you, but make allowance for their doubting, too.

- Max Ehrmann said, as far as possible, we should strive to be on good terms with all persons, speaking our truth quietly and clearly, listening to others, even to the dull and the ignorant, for they, too, have their story.

- Jesus of Nazareth said, "One does not live by bread alone." People need a higher purpose for living than simply to survive.

- We should never give up. Jesus said, "Ask, and it will be given you; search, and you will find; knock, and the door will be opened for you."

- Whoever dies with the most toys, still dies.

- We should all strive to live a good life, for we are all role models.

- Neither death, nor life, nor angels, nor rulers, nor things present, nor things to come, nor powers, nor height, nor depth, nor anything else in all creation, will be able to separate us from the love of God.

- I believe that God is the ultimate source of life and that to worship God we must live fully, share deeply, and give love away without stopping to count the cost.

- Ralph Waldo Emerson said to know even one life has breathed easier because we have lived is to have succeeded.

- The best part of any religion is in every other religion.

- Robert Hastings said there is no station, no one place to arrive. The true joy of life is the trip.

- The prophet Micah said God requires us to act justly, to love mercy, and to be humble.

- Jesus said we should love our neighbour as ourself.

- Love is the answer for we are all one people.

- Shakespeare said if you are true to yourself, you can never be false to anyone else.

- Before you quit because something isn't perfect, you should stay and try to improve it.

- Whitney Griswold said self-respect comes to us when we realize that, knowing the right thing, we have done it, and knowing the truth, we have spoken it.

- Cliff Moase says pastoral care trumps theology.

- Maya Angelou said people will forget what you said, people will forget what you did, but people will never forget how you made them feel.

Stoicism is a school of philosophy originally founded in Greece in the third century BC but adapted by many people since. According to its teachings, the path to happiness for people is found in accepting the moment as it presents itself, using one's mind to understand the world, and doing one's part in nature's plan by working fairly with others to improve the world in which we find ourselves. In addition to being able practitioners of their religions or philosophies, whatever those might have been, in my opinion, all the good people were Stoics! I might do my next speech on Stoicism!

R.P.

ABOUT THE AUTHOR

Rob Peck has seventy-five years of life experience and over forty years of public speaking experience, which he brings to this helpful how to.

In his first twenty-five years Rob travelled a lot. In the last fifty years not so much. Over the years he has sought out supportive communities who have helped him with the challenges that life inevitably brings to us all. Those communities have included family, church, neighbourhood friends, classmates from school, and Toastmasters International, a non-profit educational organization that teaches public speaking and leadership skills through a worldwide network of clubs.

Reflecting on life and the art of public speaking, Rob saw how his views had evolved over the last three decades, and decided to share that knowledge and expertise with a wider audience. He wants to encourage every reader to consider what's important in their life, and to learn how to express that in public.

Rob lives in Toronto with his wife, Julia. Their daughter, Jennifer, and her husband currently live with them as well. Though they have no pets, they do have a host of goldfish in their backyard pond.

CPSIA information can be obtained
at www.ICGtesting.com
Printed in the USA
BVHW092345270822
645634BV00004B/8

9 781039 132214